Help Me Believe in the Power of the Cross

Lord's Supper Meditations

by Joshua Welch

ONE STONE
BIBLICAL RESOURCES

Published by:
One Stone Press
979 Lovers Lane
Bowling Green, KY 42103

Printed in the United States of America

ISBN 13: 978-1-941422-75-5

www.onestone.com

Dedication

To my grandfather, Robert Welch, who was always meticulous in studying the finer points of Scripture. His Lord's Supper teaching connecting Noah to Jesus when I was a teen first opened my eyes and my curiosity to the typological nature of God's saving plan through the generations. His teaching is greatly missed, but his example in my younger years continues to be a powerful, personal motivator to mine the riches of God's Word and bring its treasures to light for others to see.

Contents

MEDITATION 1

Jesus, the True Light

In the New Testament, Paul says of the Christian, "...if anyone is in Christ, he is a new creation; old things have passed away; behold, all things have become new" (2 Corinthians 5:17). It is amazing to think that just as the Word was present at the physical creation in the beginning, He also helps us become a new creation today (Genesis 1:1; John 1:1-4). In fact, the creation story paints a preparatory picture of our own new creation. From it, we find a template for our own redemption and salvation in Christ.

Consider, what was the status of the earth before God touched it with the power of His creative energy? Genesis 1:2 says, "The earth was without form, and void; and darkness was on the face of the deep." Now, think of what we were before Christ came and changed our formless, purposeless lives. We were without hope (Ephesians 2:12). We were under the power of darkness (Colossians 1:13). We were living a life without purpose. We existed, but we had not yet been truly formed into whom God knew we could be.

So, on Day One of creation, what was first inserted onto the earth to put an end to the darkness? Genesis 1:3-4 says, "Then God said, 'Let there be light'; and there was light. And God saw the light, that it was good; and God divided the light from the darkness." Notice God never refers to the darkness as "good"—only the light (1:4). Likewise, what is it God inserts in our lives today to put an end to Satan's darkness and our sinful situation? Paul answers when he writes, "...God who commanded light to shine out of darkness...has shone in our hearts to give the light of the knowledge of the glory of God in the face of Jesus Christ" (2 Corinthians 4:6).

For this reason, the Scriptures constantly remind us Jesus is "the Light of the world" (John 8:12). John uses this imagery more in his gospel than the other gospel authors. From the very introduction of his gospel he writes of Jesus, "In Him was life, and the life was the light of men. And the light shines in the darkness, and the darkness did not comprehend it...That was the true Light which gives light to every man coming into the world" (John 1:4-5, 9). Jesus reminded, "A little while longer the light is with you. Walk while you have the light, lest darkness overtake you; he who walks in darkness does not know where he is going. While you have the light, believe in the light, that you may become sons of light" (12:35-36).

These references remind us God has been planning our redemption since before the foundation of the world (Ephesians 1:4). Literally, from the first day of creation, we can see shadows of Jesus in the light that was first cast upon the earth's formless void. May we, as His new creation, always remember the darkness we have left behind, thanks to the sacrifice of Jesus, as we follow the Light and live as light in the kingdom of light.

MEDITATION 2

Jesus, Crushing Satan's Power

Just after Adam and Eve sinned in the Garden of Eden, God pronounced a curse upon all guilty parties. Yet, included in His curse of the serpent was a glimmer of hope in the midst of the darkest moment in human history. That hope is found in Genesis 3:15:

> "And I will put enmity
> Between you and the woman,
> And between your seed and her seed;
> He shall bruise you on the head,
> And you shall bruise him on the heel."

This divine promise contains the first verbal indication to mankind that man's fall into sin would not be an unsolvable dilemma. God predicts a solution and it has much to do with why we gather at the Lord's Table. Notice a few aspects of the prediction.

First of all, this passage predicts a hostile relationship between the serpent and the woman. Keep in mind, the cursed woman was Eve. Eve's name means "the mother of all the living" (Genesis 3:20). Thus, God predicts a warlike atmosphere between not only the serpent and his progeny but also of Eve and her seed. Indeed, we are still, due to sin, in the midst of that war with Satan today (cp. Romans 16:20).

Secondly, this passage predicts a seed would one day put an end to the war. Eve may have thought her firstborn, Cain, was that seed. She exclaims at Cain's birth, "I have acquired a man from the Lord" (4:1). She knew the seed to overcome Satan's curse would be a man, as verse 15 says

9

"He shall…" However, Cain failed in this role. He worked as Satan's servant rather than his adversary. The Scriptures declare another seed as the promised one—Jesus. At the proper time, "God sent forth His Son, born of a woman, born under the law, to redeem…" (Galatians 4:4-5).

Additionally, we learn from Genesis 3:15 this seed would be dealt a temporary wound, likened to a bruised heel. The picture here leaves the door open to recovery. Men can be dealt a blow to the heel in battle and, in time, recover to full strength again. Yet, a shot or fierce blow to the head may be fatal. Jesus, when He died on the cross, was only dealt a temporary wound. He overcame death and rose from the grave to rule on His throne. His wound was temporary.

Yet, thankfully, the serpent is dealt a fatal wound. The seed of woman would bruise his head. A serpent whose head is crushed is destroyed. This is exactly what Jesus did to the serpent's power by His sacrificial death on the cross. Hebrews 2:14 says, "Inasmuch then as the children have partaken of flesh and blood, He Himself likewise shared in the same, that through death He might destroy him who had the power of death, that is, the devil…" As we consider the Lord's death, may we thank God His Son has waged the war, He has paid the price for sin, and He has defeated Satan's power over us by His death.

MEDITATION 3

Jesus, Covering Man's Sin

When Adam and Eve were first placed in the Garden of Eden and joined together as husband and wife, the text says, "they were both naked, the man and his wife, and were not ashamed" (Genesis 2:25). That particular note anticipates what would happen to Adam and Eve. After their first sin, they realize something very fundamental about themselves. Genesis 3:7 says, "Then the eyes of both of them were opened, and **they knew that they were naked**; and they sewed fig leaves together and made themselves coverings."

Apparently, their homemade fig leaf clothing was not adequate. After the curse, the text informs us, "Also for Adam and his wife the Lord God made tunics of skin, and clothed them" (Genesis 3:21). Several points have often been made from this text. Anthropologically, it is the beginning of clothing in human life. Some would argue it is the beginning of a standard of modesty which requires the covering of our nakedness. Yet, it is also noted this is the first time we see the death of an animal. Furthermore, God Himself must have sacrificed the animal to provide an appropriate covering for man's nakedness with these tunics of skin.

Some see no connection in this response to the first sin and in what our Lord does for us today in response to sin. Yet, the Scriptures make a few points clear to us which are eerily similar to this passage and are worthy of meditation.

First of all, like Adam and Eve, we are all "naked and open to the eyes of Him to whom we must give account" (Hebrews 4:13). Nakedness does refer to being unclothed or ill-clad in Scripture but it is also a metaphor for sin (cp. Revelation 3:17).

Secondly, like the first couple, we cannot ourselves cover our nakedness appropriately. Isaiah says, "we are all like an unclean thing, and all our righteousnesses are like filthy rags; we all fade as a leaf, and our iniquities, like the wind, have taken us away" (64:6). While we may try to use our own good works and righteousness as a covering for sin, Paul says salvation is, "...not of works, lest anyone should boast" (Ephesians 2:8-9). Thus, we find ourselves in a predicament we cannot fix by ourselves or by our works.

Nevertheless, like Adam and Eve, God has taken steps to take care of the problem for us. With the first pair, it took the death of an animal, one Adam had named himself, to cover their nakedness (cp. Genesis 2:19-20). With man, it took the sacrificial death of God's own Son to provide a covering for our sin. For this reason, it is important to be clothed with Christ. He is our sin covering. Galatians 3:26-27 says, "For you are all sons of God through faith in Christ Jesus. For all of you who were baptized into Christ have clothed yourselves with Christ." In Adam, we sorrow at the sin and death he brings (1 Corinthians 15:21-22). Yet in Christ, we rejoice that all shall be made alive through the resurrection of Christ and we celebrate His blood shed to cover our sins on the Lord's Day.

MEDITATION 4

Jesus, Better Than Abel

"**R**ighteous Abel" is spoken of very highly in the pages of Scripture, even by Jesus (Matthew 23:35; Hebrews 11:4). The story of this first martyr of the Bible is told in Genesis 4, where he is hated so fiercely by his brother Cain, he is murdered in the field (Genesis 4:8).

After Abel's murder, the Lord memorably asks jealous Cain, "Where is Abel your brother?" (Genesis 4:9).

Cain dismissively answers, "I do not know. Am I my brother's keeper?" (4:9).

God replies, "What have you done? The voice of your brother's blood cries out to Me from the ground. So now you are cursed from the earth, which has opened its mouth to receive your brother's blood from your hand. When you till the ground, it shall no longer yield its strength to you. A fugitive and a vagabond you shall be on the earth" (Genesis 4:10-12). There is a strong indication in God's response that bloodshed is not to be taken lightly or dismissively.

After Cain hears of God's sentencing for his actions he complains, "My punishment is greater than I can bear!" (Genesis 4:13).

There are interesting similarities between Jesus and Abel. Abel was a keeper of sheep while Jesus is the Good Shepherd (Genesis 4:2; John 10:11). Abel sacrificed one of his firstborn lambs just as Jesus, God's firstborn, is called the Lamb of God (Genesis 4:4; John 1:29). Abel was hated by his brother, just as Jesus was hated by many of his own brethren (Genesis 4:5-8; John 1:11). Abel shed his blood in the field and Jesus shed his as well, as he was crucified on the cross of Calvary (Genesis 4:8, 10; Hebrews 10:27-28).

Despite these similarities, the blood of Jesus "speaks better things than that of Abel" (Hebrews 12:24). But, why would the blood of Jesus speak better things? How? In the Genesis text, the blood of Abel cried out for vengeance and led to a fugitive lifestyle for Cain, separated from his brethren. Cain is estranged, punished, and marked because of the blood of Abel. Yet, through the blood of Jesus, we receive remission of sins and now have the right to become children of God and united in fellowship with Christ (John 1:12).

As we sup from the cup at the Lord's Table, may we be forever grateful of the blood our Lord shed. Because of His blood, He is merciful to our unrighteousness and our sins and lawless deeds He will remember no more (Hebrews 8:12). By His shed blood He has appeared to put away sin by the sacrifice of Himself. Abel's blood never washed away a single sin. Yet Christ was offered once to bear the sins of many (Hebrews 9:28). Abel's blood cried out for vengeance, but the blood of Jesus is a symbol of God's mercy towards us so we may be united as brethren.

MEDITATION 5

Jesus, the Ark of Safety

One of the more well-known accounts of the Old Testament is of Noah and the ark he built in preparation for the global flood (Genesis 6-9). According to Peter, some of the events with Noah and his ark typify and foreshadow the salvation we find in Jesus Christ (1 Peter 3:18-22). Consider a few ways.

First of all, in the days of Noah, the world was headed for destruction. Genesis 6:7 says, "So the Lord said, 'I will destroy man whom I have created from the face of the earth, both man and beast, creeping things and birds of the air, for I am sorry that I have made them'" (NKJV). Today, man finds himself in a similar situation. Our sins bring God's displeasure. Romans 2:5 says, "But in accordance with your hardness and your impenitent heart you are treasuring up for yourself wrath in the day of wrath and revelation of the righteous judgment of God..." This verse makes our situation seem hopeless if God were all justice, but thankfully, we serve a God of grace, too.

This grace was bestowed upon Noah during the days of the flood. Genesis 6:8 says, "But Noah found favor in the eyes of the Lord" (6:9, NASB). Today, like Noah, we should be thankful God has offered His grace despite the fact we have been a disappointment by our sins. "For the wages of sin is death, but the free gift of God is eternal life in Christ Jesus our Lord" (Romans 6:23).

Yet, how does God offer this great gift to us? In the days of Noah, God bestowed His grace upon Noah by warning him of the coming destruction and giving him the means to be saved from the global flood—the building of the ark. Hebrews 11:7 says, "By faith Noah, after he was warned about what was not yet seen and motivated by godly fear, built an ark to deliver his family" (HCSB). Just as the ark was God's means of deliverance, the blood of Jesus Christ is God's means to deliver us. 1 Peter 3:18 says, "For Christ also died for sins once for all, the just for the unjust, so that He might bring us to God, having been put to death in the flesh, but made alive in the spirit…" (NASB). The ark may have been Noah's place of safety, but, Jesus, is our means of deliverance today. Just as Noah's salvation began as the waters surrounded the ark, so our new life is initiated when we are baptized into our Savior, Jesus Christ (1 Peter 3:21-22; cp. Romans 6:1-6).

The disbelieving world may have found Noah's salvation via an ark an unfathomable tale (cp. Matthew 24:37-39). Yet, with every hammer of every nail, Noah was warning the lost world of the salvation to come. Likewise, some may see the message of the cross as foolishness, but every time we eat this bread and drink this cup to memorialize our Lord's means of rescue, we "proclaim the Lord's death until He comes" (1 Corinthians 1:18; 11:26). May we continue to eat and drink of the Lord until the rough seas of this life have subsided and the door is opened to a new heavens and a new earth.

MEDITATION 6

Jesus, the Seed of Abraham

The main theme of the entire Bible can be summarized in the three major promises God made to Abraham in Genesis 12.

In the first promise, God tells Abraham he is going to put him in "a land that I will show you" (Genesis 12:1). Indeed, one of the major themes of the Old Testament is Israel's claim to their land. The exodus out of Egypt is for the purpose of entering Canaan's land. The wilderness wandering is a delay prior to entering the land through the conquest of Joshua. The captivity illustrates the sadness of losing the land. The return from captivity by a remnant of Israel is a joyous occasion as God restores the land to His people. It was in the land of Israel where Jesus was born, did the bulk of His ministry, and would die.

In the second promise, God tells Abraham, "I will make you a great nation" (Genesis 12:2). The history of that nation, the nation of Israel, is traced from the time of the patriarchs all the way to the time of Jesus Christ.

In the third promise, God assures Abraham, "in you all the families of the earth shall be blessed" (Genesis 12:3). Later, God reaffirms this promise saying, "In your seed all the nations of the earth shall be blessed…" (Genesis 22:18). This promise did not just involve the people of Israel, but all families and all nations. So, how did it come true?

In the very first verse of the gospels, Matthew says of Jesus he was "the Son of David, the Son of Abraham…" (Matthew 1:1). These two phrases would have great significance to a Jewish reader. As we consider the Abrahamic promise, they have great meaning to us as well.

In Acts 3, Peter explains how God blessed all nations through the seed of Abraham. That explanation involves Jesus, the Son of Abraham. Verses 25 and 26 say, "You are sons of the prophets, and of the covenant which God made with our fathers, saying to Abraham, 'And in your seed all the families of the earth shall be blessed.' To you first, God, having raised up His Servant Jesus, sent Him to bless you, in turning away every one of you from your iniquities."

Today, we can enjoy the same blessings as any other family or nation because of the seed of Abraham, Jesus Christ, who died for our sins, was buried and rose again. He died in order to do something about our iniquity, our sin (cp. Isaiah 53:5). As we partake of the bread and fruit of the vine, we rejoice that God has kept His promise and blessed us through Jesus Christ, our broken, bruised and blood-stained Savior. He has blessed us not to be part of a physical nation, but part of a holy nation, His church (1 Peter 2:9). As Christians, we enjoy not a physical land, but the hope of being part of a new heavens and new earth in His eternal kingdom (2 Peter 3:13). What great blessings to consider as we remember the great benefits of our Lord's broken body and shed blood!

MEDITATION 7

Jesus, Our King and Priest

In Genesis 14 we are introduced to Melchizedek. Melchizedek is the key person of comparison with Jesus throughout the entire text of Hebrews 7.

A cursory reading of the Genesis text ought to bring to mind several words also connected with Jesus.

> "Then Melchizedek king of Salem brought out bread and wine; he was the priest of God Most High. And he blessed him and said: 'Blessed be Abram of God Most High, Possessor of heaven and earth; And blessed be God Most High, Who has delivered your enemies into your hand.' And he gave him a tithe of all" (Genesis 14:18-20).

Immediately, words like "king," "bread," "wine," and "priest" should also make us think of the Messiah. Furthermore, Melchizedek shows up again in the Old Testament text. Psalm 110:4 says, "The Lord has sworn and will not relent, 'You are a priest forever according to the order of Melchizedek.'" This descriptive word "forever" makes the case even more captivating. No Levitical priest was ever a priest forever. This is only a quality which could be ascribed to an eternal God. This is exactly the case made in Hebrews 7:3 for Jesus Christ. Consider a few brief contrasts…

First, Jesus, like Melchizedek, is indeed a king (Luke 23:2), but not over a limited locale. Jesus is the King of kings (Revelation 17:14).

Second, Jesus is a king who brings peace (the word *Salem* means peace). Isaiah prophesied about the Prince of Peace (Isaiah 9:6; cp. Ephesians 2:13-14).

Third, Jesus is also a priest who acts as a Mediator between God and men (1 Timothy 2:5). He is a high priest, after the order of Melchizedek, who served under a different law than required by Moses (Hebrews 7:14-15). This, in fact, is the main point of the Hebrew writer's comparison between the priesthood of Melchizedek and Jesus (8:1).

After the victory of Abram, Melchizedek comes to bless Abram bringing out bread and wine (Genesis 14:18). Matthew 26:26-28 records the institution of the Lord's Supper and the bread and fruit of the vine which was shared to commemorate Christ's body and His blood. There is a reason Paul calls it "the cup of blessing" (1 Corinthians 10:16). It is through His blood, that Christ has made a new covenant with His people (Hebrews 7:22). He has battled Satan, won the victory and blessed the faithful in His sacrifice.

Each of these comparisons are simple reminders God was foreshadowing Jesus, our forever Priest and King, in the person of righteous Melchizedek. The bread and wine are not just arbitrary details in the Melchizedek passage of Genesis 14. They are purposefully planned elements made more meaningful in Christ as we commemorate the great future blessing of our victory through our King and High Priest, Jesus Christ!

MEDITATION 8

Jesus, God's Only Son

The Genesis 22 account of Abraham's willingness to sacrifice Isaac brings immediate reminders of God allowing His Son to be sacrificed on the cross. Consider the similarities between Abraham in Genesis 22 and God's gift of His Son, Jesus…

- Both are willing to give their only son (Genesis 22:2).

- Isaac is rescued three days later, Jesus is resurrected (22:4; Matthew 28:1)

- Isaac lays on the wood (22:6, 9), Jesus is nailed to a cross (Matthew 27:35).

- God promises Abraham a lamb (22:8), Jesus is the Lamb (John 1:29).

- Sacrifices a ram instead of Isaac (22:12-13), Jesus dies for us (Romans 8:32).

- Promises to bless all nations (22:18; cp. Matthew 26:28; Luke 24:47).

To some, this may just seem like a few incidental similarities were it not for a few more details. First of all, consider the fact God's choice of where Abraham would sacrifice Isaac was intentional. Twice in the Genesis account we are told God picked out the exact mountain upon which the sacrifice would be offered (see Genesis 22:3, 9). This exact locale is called Mt. Moriah (Genesis 22:2, 14). Later, Abraham would call it *"Jehovah-Jireh,"* translated as "the Lord will provide." What was significant about this place?

Fast forward the clock a few hundred years and we see Mt. Moriah mentioned again in the text of Scripture, this time with David. David is purchasing a site on Moriah, at great expense, so an altar can be built for burnt offerings and sacrifices to God (2 Samuel 24:24-25; 1 Chronicles 21:25). This site would be the locale where Solomon would later build the temple and numerous sacrifices of lambs were slaughtered as burnt offerings on the altar (2 Chronicles 3:1).

Now, think. Abraham is willing to offer the costly gift of his own Son on Mt. Moriah. David pays a costly amount to make an offering on Mt. Moriah. Solomon builds a lavish temple and permanent altar on Mt. Moriah for burnt offerings. Then, as we come to Jesus Christ, the Passover Lamb of God, He offers Himself on the same mount, now called Mt. Calvary, for man's sins.

Jesus once said to the Jews, "Your father Abraham rejoiced to see My day, and he saw it and was glad" (John 8:56). Why would Abraham rejoice to see the day of Jesus? Because Jesus fulfilled the promises given to the fathers, such as Genesis 22:14, and was the final Lamb God would ever need to provide on Mt. Calvary for the sins of the world!

This is not coincidence. It was intentionally given as evidence to believe what John so succinctly states in John 3:16, "For God so loved the world that He gave His only begotten Son, that whoever believes in Him should not perish but have everlasting life." Like Abraham, may we rejoice that the Lord has kept His promise and provided a Lamb to atone for our sins. Because of this gift, we remember His sin offering on the first day of the week.

MEDITATION 9

The Father of the Faithful

After Abram had gone years without a child, God spoke to him, saying, "'...one who will come forth from your own body, he shall be your heir.' And He took him outside and said, 'Now look toward the heavens, and count the stars, if you are able to count them.' And He said to him, 'So shall your descendants be'" (Genesis 15:4-5).

This promise was getting harder and harder for Abram to believe with each passing year. He was getting older and still no male child had been borne to him. In fact, he was so old, the Hebrew writer calls him "as good as dead" (Hebrews 11:11-12). Yet, God kept His promise to Abram and, indeed, Isaac was born, then Jacob, then Jacob's twelve sons (the twelve tribes of Israel) and then the great and mighty nation of Israel.

This story may sound familiar. Abram found his old age a stumbling block. The hope that a mighty nation could be borne from his frail flesh seemed to be slowly extinguishing with each passing day. Yet, God was stronger than Abram's weakness.

Like Abram, Jesus is the founder of a holy nation (1 Peter 2:9). Jesus was not just as good as dead though—He *was* dead (1 Corinthians 15:1-3). When Jesus expired on the cross, it seemed as though all hope was gone for this man who claimed to be a Savior. The disciples were full of dreadful doubt and tears. Yet, three days later, Jesus arose from the dead (1 Peter 1:19-21). With the help of His twelve apostles, His nation of disciples grew as the book of Acts records. However, to many Jews, the thought of a crucified Savior was a stumbling block (1 Corinthians 1:23; 1 Peter 2:8). Nevertheless, just as God used the weakness of Abraham as proof of His power, He used the deadness of Jesus as proof, too. So, to us, the message of the cross is the power of God (1 Corinthians 1:18).

To the world, it may seem foolish to remember Jesus through the emblems of the Lord's Supper on a weekly basis. Yet, these emblems representing His body and His blood are reminders of how God can take our weakness, our sins, and our spiritual deadness and grant to us new life through His power and through His Son, Jesus Christ (see Romans 8:11). We know He can lift us from the deadness of our sins, because God raised Jesus from His death.

So, as we look at the same stars Abram once viewed, may we praise God that we have the honor of being one of the innumerable descendants of Jesus Christ. As Peter once said, "For the promise is to you and to your children, and to all who are afar off, as many as the Lord our God will call" (Acts 2:39). Two millennia later, it is truly a blessing to be part of God's mighty nation. The world may seem to have us outnumbered. The odds may seem to be against us. But, these emblems are reminders of God's covenant to take each person's hopeless situation and turn it into a victory.

MEDITATION 10

God Will Provide a Lamb

In the Genesis account of Abraham's call to sacrifice Isaac, we learn that Isaac was spared from the sacrifice. Instead, Abraham explains, "God Himself will provide the lamb for the burnt offering, my son" (Genesis 22:8).

Upon many occasions, God has required a lamb as a sacrifice to provide atonement for the sins of the people.

- He called for a lamb to be offered for each household at the first Passover to spare the firstborn from wrath (Exodus 12:3, 5, 13).

- God called for a lamb during the burnt offerings so the animals could be offered on his behalf to make atonement (Leviticus 1:1-2, 4, 10, 13).

- In 1 Samuel 7, when the people admitted their sin, it was Samuel who "took a suckling lamb and offered it as a whole burnt offering to the Lord" (7:6, 9, 14).

In each of these instances, God graciously provides mercy through the death of a lamb. Yet, the book of Hebrews tells us these sacrifices were only a shadow of the good things to come (10:1). Unfortunately, "in those sacrifices there is a reminder of sins every year. For it is not possible that the blood of bulls and goats could take away sins" (10:3-4). Fortunately, God did provide a Lamb who could take away sin—permanently.

Each of those sacrifices were only painting a shadowy picture pointing ahead to what is finally fulfilled in Jesus. While Abraham did spare his son, God "did not spare His own Son, but delivered Him up for us all" (Romans 8:32). Why does this matter? Because Jesus provided the atoning sacrifice for our sins. As John once stated after looking at Jesus, "Behold! The Lamb of God who takes away the sin of the world!" (John 1:29, NKJV).

So, we now have a new covenant in which we share, through Jesus (Matthew 26:28). It is not like the old covenant, which required an annual sacrifice of the blood of bulls and goats. We now have been washed through the blood sacrifice of Jesus Christ, the Son of God, who died for us. As we sup, we show our appreciation for the new relationship we have with God through the Lamb who was provided for us.

MEDITATION 11

Jesus, Assumed to Be Dead

There are so many similarities between Jacob's son Joseph and Jesus that it is hard to avoid the typological comparisons. For example…

- Both are shepherds (Genesis 37:2; John 10:11, 14).

- Both are loved by their father (Genesis 37:3; Matthew 3:17).

- Both are hated by their brethren (Genesis 37:4-5; John 15:25).

- Both are rejected and envied for claiming pre-eminence (Genesis 37:5-11; Luke 19:14; Mark 15:10).

- Both are conspired against by their brethren (Genesis 37:18; Matthew 27:1).

- Both are stripped of their clothing (Genesis 37:23; Matthew 27:28).

- Both are sold for silver (Genesis 37:28; Matthew 26:15; 27:9).

- Both are exalted and willing to forgive and redeem their brethren after their suffering (Genesis 50:18-21; Hebrews 2:9-10).

This list of similarities could go on and on. While the New Testament never specially notes these comparisons, it is hard not to be impressed. As we assemble together to "proclaim the Lord's death till He comes" (1 Corinthians 11:26) notice one more interesting comparison—the presumed death of Joseph himself.

After Joseph is sold into slavery to the Ishmaelites, his brothers realize they must hide their mischievous doings from their father, Jacob. So, instead of telling the real story, they dip Joseph's tunic in blood and let Jacob's worst fears take over as they come home to show him the blood-stained garment (Genesis 37:31-32). Jacob presumes, "It is my son's tunic. A wild beast has devoured him. Without doubt Joseph is torn to pieces" (Genesis 37:32-33). Of course, years later, Jacob learns Joseph is not dead. He is now a ruler in Egypt and the Savior of Israel from the famine (cp. Genesis 45:25-28; 46:29-30).

This should sound very familiar. At the death of Jesus, His disciples and closest friends were filled with sadness, presuming Jesus had died, never to be seen again (Mark 16:10-11). Yet, days later, Jesus presented Himself alive. His presence revived His deflated disciples with a living hope. It ignited an inextinguishable flame of passion for the Lord as they proclaimed Him the rest of their lives (John 20:19-20, 28-31).

On this Lord's day, we celebrate Jesus, the one who was merely presumed to be dead. Yet as Peter would later say of His death, "it was not possible that He should be held by it" (Acts 2:24). Why was it not possible for Jesus to stay dead? Simple. God had made a promise. Like Joseph's dream, God had promised Jesus would one day reign on a throne as Lord (Acts 2:32, 36). God keeps His promises. Now, He reigns and we celebrate His death because it enables us to rejoice in the hope of new life He offers.

MEDITATION 12

Jesus, Worshipping at Death

Hebrews 11:21 says, "By faith Jacob, when he was dying, blessed each of the sons of Joseph, and worshiped, leaning on the top of his staff." This is a short text with a much fuller context if we go to the original account in the book of Genesis.

In Genesis 47, Jacob is living in Egypt after being rescued from famine and reunited with his son Joseph. Jacob is old and dying. So he asks his son to make a promise: "Please do not bury me in Egypt, but let me lie with my fathers; you shall carry me out of Egypt and bury me in their burial place." Joseph agrees to the conditions and, in response, "Israel bowed himself on the head of his bed" (47:30-31)—an act of worship.

Some would argue the staff mentioned in Hebrews 11:21 is in fact, the head of the bed. Genesis 48:2 says, when Joseph came with his two sons, Israel strengthened himself and sat up on the bed before blessing the sons of Joseph and praising the "God who has fed me all my life long to this day" (48:15). Despite the near impending death of Jacob, his tone is still hopeful. He says to Joseph, "Behold, I am dying, but God will be with you and bring you back to the land of your fathers" (48:21).

This account is plain enough, but the Hebrew writer wanted us to see a deeper shade of meaning. He comments in Hebrews 12:1-2 that all of this great cloud of witnesses were looking unto Jesus. In other words, somehow, their lives point us to a greater fulfillment of faith in Jesus Christ. How might Jacob give us a faint picture of Jesus?

First, Jacob did not want his bones left in Egypt. There was a home that meant much more to him than Egypt—Canaan's land. He wanted his body taken home. Likewise, the body of Jesus was not left on this sin-filled earth. Peter preached, "...His soul was not left in Hades, nor did His flesh see corruption" (Acts 2:31). Jesus ascended.

Secondly, Jacob worshipped, even at death, as he considered the promise of Joseph (Genesis 47:31). Jacob worshipped while propped up on his head board, but Jesus worshipped while nailed to the cross. In Luke 23:46 Jesus says, "'Father, into Your hands I commit My spirit.' Having said this, He breathed His last." Why could Jesus confidently worship at death? He had confidence in His Father who keeps His promises!

Thirdly, Jacob blessed his sons and grandsons at his death. The context of Genesis 48-49 is about Jacob's blessing. Likewise, Jesus blessed us in His death, for our sins, on the cross. Peter preached, "God, having raised up His Servant Jesus, sent Him to bless you, in turning away every one of you from your iniquities" (Acts 3:26).

Jacob had hope in the promises of God after death. Jesus had hope in the promises of God at death. Likewise, our hope is an anchor of the soul we celebrate at this memorial of the death of our Lord, who worshipped even as He expired. Praise God!

MEDITATION 13

Jesus, the Lamb Without Blemish

The prophet Malachi once rebuked the people of Israel saying, "You offer defiled food on My altar, but say, 'In what way have we defiled You?'…And when you offer the blind as a sacrifice, is it not evil? And when you offer the lame and sick, is it not evil? Offer it then to your governor! Would he be pleased with you? Would he accept you favorably?" (Malachi 1:7-8)

Clearly, the Lord was not pleased with Israel's offerings from the most worthless animals of their flock. It would be the modern-day equivalent of serving an honored guest roadkill off the highway for dinner. Later, Malachi would add,

> "'…you bring the stolen, the lame, and the sick; Thus you bring an offering! Should I accept this from your hand?' Says the Lord. 'But cursed be the deceiver who has in his flock a male, and takes a vow, but sacrifices to the Lord what is blemished—For I am a great King,' says the Lord of hosts, 'And My name is to be feared among the nations'" (Malachi 1:13-14).

The principle behind Malachi's rebuke is clear. The King of kings deserves the best man has to offer and not the leftovers. Yet, how often is that how some serve and give to the Lord? Not only was this a violation of the specific commands God had given concerning offerings, but it also mars the very image these sacrifices were to portray.

In the book of Exodus, when the Lord first gave instructions concerning the offering of the Passover Lamb, God stated, "Your lamb shall be without blemish, a male of the first year. You may take it from the sheep or from the goats" (Exodus 12:5). The phrase "without blemish" is repeated often as the Levitical offerings are instituted (see Leviticus 1:3, 10; 3:1, 6, 9; 4:3, 23, 28, 32; 5:15, 18; 6:6; 9:2-3; 14:10; 22:19, 21; 23:12, 15, 18). This phrase is not just a coincidence, but an intentional pattern of repetition for our notice.

Peter noted the fulfillment of what these offerings were to foreshadow as he wrote of the unblemished Jesus Christ saying, "you were not redeemed with corruptible things, like silver or gold, from your aimless conduct received by tradition from your fathers, but with the precious blood of Christ, as of a lamb without blemish and without spot" (1 Peter 1:18-19). The people of Israel were to give their unblemished offerings because it was symbolic of the unblemished Son of God whom God Himself gave on behalf of the world.

As we gather around this table, may we be filled with thanks that God gave the very best heaven had to offer for our sins. Each offering from Israel was to resemble God's ultimate offering for all men, for all time. May we learn from the mistakes of Israel and imitate the gracious offering of our Almighty God as we serve Him daily and reflect upon the memorial of His unblemished sacrifice who was broken only for us.

MEDITATION 14

Jesus Saves From Wrath Through Blood

When God instituted the Passover, he required Israel to take "some of the blood and put it on the two doorposts and on the lintel of the houses where they eat it" (Exodus 12:7). There was a promise connected to this application of the blood. The Lord said, "Now the blood shall be a sign for you on the houses where you are. And when I see the blood, I will pass over you; and the plague shall not be on you to destroy you when I strike the land of Egypt" (Exodus 12:13).

Later in the chapter we read of those whom the Lord did not "Passover" as the text says, "And it came to pass at midnight that the Lord struck all the firstborn in the land of Egypt, from the firstborn of Pharaoh who sat on his throne to the firstborn of the captive who was in the dungeon, and all the firstborn of livestock. So Pharaoh rose in the night, he, all his servants, and all the Egyptians; and there was a great cry in Egypt, for there was not a house where there was not one dead" (Exodus 12:29-30).

The events in Egypt on this day were both marvelously powerful and tragically painful. To Israel, this event initiates their wonderful deliverance from Egyptian bondage. Yet, to Egypt, these events brought about the most painful type of loss—the death of the firstborn child in every home. To Christians, this account is intended to foreshadow so much more. 1 Corinthians 5:7 says, "...Christ, our Passover, was sacrificed for us." Romans 5:8-9 says, "...while we were still sinners, Christ died for us. Much more then, having now been justified by His blood, we shall be saved from wrath through Him."

The Passover scene teaches some essential truths. First of all, "It is a fearful thing to fall into the hands of the living God" (Hebrews 10:31). Pharaoh should not have toyed with rebellion and learned the hard way. Secondly, God's wrath can be turned away through the blood of an unblemished sacrifice (as we see many more times in the Levitical offerings). Finally, when the blood of a perfect sacrifice was applied to the doorpost, God could grant safety to the household protected by the blood.

As we approach the Lord's Table today, to celebrate our Passover Lamb, this meal becomes more meaningful with this backdrop. God could have justly destroyed us because of our sins and rebellion. Yet, He chose instead to allow His sinless Son to be sacrificed for us. So, if the blood of Jesus Christ has been applied to our lives, through obedient faith, we can be saved from an eternal death and delivered to enjoy eternal life. Though Israel experienced a history of blood offerings, all of humanity can enjoy the blessings of the blood of Jesus Christ through His sacrifice on the cross (see Hebrews 10:28). How sad to think some refuse to share in this great memorial Supper which reminds us of how we have been saved from wrath through Jesus. There is power in the blood and safety in the household of Jesus Christ.

MEDITATION 15

Jesus, Our Passover

At the first Passover prior to the Exodus, the text says, "Then Moses called for all the elders of Israel and said to them, 'Pick out and take lambs for yourselves according to your families, and kill the Passover lamb…And you shall observe this thing as an ordinance for you and your sons forever…And it shall be, when your children say to you, 'What do you mean by this service?' that you shall say, 'It is the Passover sacrifice of the Lord, who passed over the houses of the children of Israel in Egypt when He struck the Egyptians and delivered our households.' So the people bowed their heads and worshiped" (Exodus 12:21, 24-27).

There are many words and phrases that describe God's attitude toward our sins as he forgives us. Here are a few…

- "As far as the east is from the west, so far has He **removed our transgressions from us**" (Psalm 103:12).

- "'Come now, and let us reason together,' says the Lord, '**Though your sins are like scarlet, they shall be as white as snow**; though they are red like crimson, they shall be as wool'" (Isaiah 1:18).

- "I, even I, am He who **blots out your transgressions** for My own sake; and I will **not remember your sins**" (Isaiah 43:25).

- "Who is a God like You, Pardoning iniquity and **passing over the transgression of the remnant** of His heritage?…He will again have compassion on us, and will subdue our iniquities. **You will cast all our sins into the depths of the sea**" (Micah 7:18-19).

- "For this is My blood of the new covenant, which is shed for many **for the remission of sins**" (Matthew 26:28; cp. Acts 2:38).

35

- "Repent therefore and be converted, **that your sins may be blotted out**, so that times of refreshing may come from the presence of the Lord..." (Acts 3:19).

- "Their sins and their lawless deeds **I will remember no more**" (Hebrews 10:17).

These words and phrases are all intended to provide for us a better understanding of the forgiveness of God. Yet, the literal Passover feast was a vivid picture as well. It was a memorial of the time the firstborn in Israel's houses were passed over because they were protected by the blood of a sacrificial lamb. This was not just a memorial, but a future picture of what God has done for us through Jesus Christ. We deserved death for our sins. Yet Christ, our Passover, was sacrificed for us (1 Corinthians 5:7). That concise, powerful thought ought to resonate as one of many poignant pictures God gives us to remember the forgiveness He provides through the Son. Jesus is our Passover. He gave His life so we might live.

MEDITATION 16

Jesus, the Bread of Life

In the Old Testament, the people of Israel wandered in the wilderness without a sustainable food supply. Exodus 16:4 relays God's miraculous solution: "Then the Lord said to Moses, 'Behold, I will rain bread from heaven for you. And the people shall go out and gather a certain quota every day...'" While this miracle occurred in the days of Moses, Jesus gives the glory to God saying, "Most assuredly, I say to you, Moses did not give you the bread from heaven, but My Father gives you the true bread from heaven" (John 6:32).

However, Jesus takes this bread theme a step further when he adds, "For the bread of God is He who comes down from heaven and gives life to the world...I am the bread of life. He who comes to Me shall never hunger..." (John 6:33, 35). This powerful contrast is an indication from Jesus that the manna from heaven was a foreshadowing of something greater from heaven God would provide—His own Son!

While Jesus only specifically mentions the manna episode in the John 6 comparison, there are many ways the Old Testament scriptures foreshadow the life of Jesus through bread. For example, Jesus was born in Bethlehem, meaning "the house of bread." Fittingly, the bread of God is born in the house of bread.

A picture of Jesus is also found in the tabernacle's showbread in Exodus 25 (see also Hebrews 9:2, 9). Exodus 25:30 says, "And you shall set the showbread on the table before Me always." This showbread was representative of Jesus, our eternal Mediator and Advocate who sustains us by His mediation (1 John 2:1-2).

Additionally, Jesus, the bread of life, was also foreshadowed in the grain offerings required under Old Testament law (as Hebrews 9 alludes to). Leviticus 2 refers to those offerings and they give us a picture of Jesus in the following ways:

• The grain offering of your firstfruits was to be grain beaten from full heads, just as Jesus, the Bread of Life, was beaten and bruised for us (Leviticus 2:14; Matthew 26:67).

• The grain offering was to be made with no leaven (a word that represents evil—see Matthew 16:6), just as Jesus was without sin for us (Leviticus 2:11; 1 Peter 2:22).

In picture after picture, God is foreshadowing His Son Jesus through bread. This bread of life descends from heaven, lives an unleavened life, is beaten and bruised and sifted through trials as our offering, and now is forever in the presence of God as our Mediator and Advocate in heaven. So, as we gather together on the Lord's day, it is fitting to partake of this unleavened bread which was both a foreshadowing of Jesus and now a memorial of His body, which was offered to feed and sustain us with life eternal. As we break this bread, may the words of the Bread of Life ring in our ears, "Take, eat; this is My body" (Matthew 26:26).

MEDITATION 17

His Sacrifice Is a Sweet Aroma

One of Noah's first acts as he departed from the ark is recorded in Genesis 8:20-21, "Then Noah built an altar to the Lord, and took of every clean animal and of every clean bird, and offered burnt offerings on the altar. And the Lord smelled a soothing aroma."

In the Levitical sacrifices, a similar response is repeated to the one we find from God after Noah's offering.

- The burnt offering would be "an offering made by fire, a sweet aroma to the Lord" (Leviticus 1:9, 13, 17).

- The grain offering would be "an offering made by fire, a sweet aroma to the Lord" (Leviticus 2:2, 9).

- The peace offering would be "an offering made by fire, a sweet aroma to the Lord" (Leviticus 3:1, 5, 16).

- The sin offerings would be burned "on the altar for a sweet aroma to the Lord" (Leviticus 4:24, 31).

In many of the phrases regarding these offerings, there is repetition and a pattern. These special offerings all look forward to a future, greater fulfillment in Christ. Christ is our atonement, our bread, our peace, our propitiation, and our trespass offering. Paul finishes out the pattern by using the same phraseology in Ephesians 5:1-2, "Therefore be imitators of God as dear children. And walk in love, as Christ also has loved us and given Himself for us, an offering and a sacrifice to God for a sweet-smelling aroma."

The similarities in Leviticus and in Ephesians 5 are not coincidental, but intentional. In the earlier Ephesian context, Paul realized we were "brought near by the blood of Christ. For He Himself is our peace..." (Ephesians 2:13-14). This is a clear reference to Jesus being our peace offering. Paul starts out his epistle to Ephesus noting how "we have redemption through His blood, the forgiveness of sins, according to the riches of His grace..." (1:7). This is a picture of Jesus as our atoning sacrifice. Later, he mentions we "were dead in trespasses and sins" (2:1), which calls to mind the sin offering and trespass offering. The importance of blood, offerings, peace and reconciliation were not new. They were familiar pictures. It was just that Jesus needed to be painted into the portrait.

What a wonderful thought for us to consider as we gather around the Lord's Table. The offering and sacrifice of Jesus—our spiritual food—is a sweet aroma to the Lord and should be to us as well. Without His voluntary sacrifice, we would have no hope for forgiveness and peace with God. As we remember His sacrifice, we ensure His offering for us was not made in vain.

MEDITATION 18

Jesus Makes Atonement

There is much imagery in the Old Testament which foreshadows what is fulfilled in Jesus Christ under the new covenant. One such picture is the Day of Atonement's sin offering made by the high priest (originally Aaron) in Leviticus 16:15-17:

> "Then he shall kill the goat of the sin offering, which is for the people, brings its blood inside the veil, do with that blood as he did with the blood of the bull, and sprinkle it on the mercy seat and before the mercy seat. So he shall make atonement for the Holy Place, because of the uncleanness of the children of Israel, and because of their transgressions, for all their sins; and so he shall do for the tabernacle of meeting which remains among them in the midst of their uncleanness. There shall be no man in the tabernacle of meeting when he goes in to make atonement in the Holy Place, until he comes out, that he may make atonement for himself, for his household, and for all the assembly of Israel."

The book of Hebrews conveys the fulfillment of many of these tabernacle pictures in Jesus Christ, our High Priest. Hebrews 9:11-12 says,

> "But Christ came as High Priest of the good things to come, with the greater and more perfect tabernacle not made with hands, that is, not of this creation. Not with the blood of goats and calves, but with His own blood He entered the Most Holy Place once for all, having obtained eternal redemption."

The Old Testament rituals were not just random requirements from an arbitrary God. They were prophetic pictures of what God planned to do through Jesus.

- The tabernacle looks to Jesus who "tabernacled" among us (John 1:14).

- The goat without blemish pictures the sinless Jesus (1 Peter 1:18-19).

- The blood shed foreshadows the high cost paid by Jesus, His own blood, to redeem sinful man (Acts 20:28).

- The mercy seat upon which the blood was poured reminds us of our propitiation (a word that means mercy seat) through Jesus (Romans 3:25).

- The once a year (Leviticus 16:34) Day of Atonement looked ahead to the once for all sacrifice of Jesus (Hebrews 9:12).

When we consider the foreshadowing of Christ in all of the minute details of the Old Testament Day of Atonement, we are truly in awe of how God has always loved us and planned to bring us back to Him through the blood of His Son! In the words of one hymn writer,

> "Guilty, vile and helpless we;
> Spotless Lamb of God was He;
> Full atonement! can it be?
> Hallelujah, what a Savior!"

Hallelujah indeed!

MEDITATION 19

Jesus, Lifted Up to Heal Mankind

To anyone who hates snakes, a frightening event occurs to the complaining children of Israel while they are in the wilderness. As a result of their sin, "the Lord sent fiery serpents among the people, and they bit the people; and many of the people of Israel died" (Numbers 21:6). However, as God's people admit their sin and cry out for mercy through their mediator Moses, a remedy is sent. We read of God's cure in Numbers 21:8-9.

> "Then the Lord said to Moses, 'Make a fiery serpent, and set it on a pole; and it shall be that everyone who is bitten, when he looks at it, shall live.' So Moses made a bronze serpent, and put it on a pole; and so it was, if a serpent had bitten anyone, when he looked at the bronze serpent, he lived" (NKJV).

This event makes its way into the gospel conversation as the prophet like Moses speaks to Nicodemus in John 3:14-15 saying, "And as Moses lifted up the serpent in the wilderness, even so must the Son of Man be lifted up, that whoever believes in Him should not perish but have eternal life."

By this comparison, Jesus sees a foreshadowing of the cross in the bronze serpent of Moses. As we gather around the Lord's table to remember our crucified Savior, it may deepen our faith in the power of the cross to consider these comparisons.

Without the brazen serpent, the consequences of Israel's sin was death (Numbers 21:6). Likewise, without the saving cross of Jesus Christ, the final "wages of sin is death, but the gift of God is eternal life in Jesus Christ our Lord" (Romans 6:23).

Yet, thankfully, the compassion and mercy of God sends a remedy for sin. God's Word descended from on high to instruct Moses concerning the cure—the brazen serpent lifted up on a pole. Likewise, the Son of Man Himself came down from heaven to serve as God's final messenger for man (John 3:13). Like the brazen serpent, he was lifted up on the cross of Calvary to save whoever believes in Him (John 3:14-16).

Finally, God instructed Moses to use an image of the very serpents who were bringing death to the people to bring salvation. Likewise, Jesus came in the likeness of sinful flesh when he came to earth as a man (Romans 8:3). Yet, God "made Him who knew no sin to be sin for us, that we might become the righteousness of God in Him" (2 Corinthians 5:21).

Without Jesus being lifted up, man would have no hope, no cure for the curse brought about by sin. Yet by the power of the cross, "Christ has redeemed us from the curse of the law, having become a curse for us" (Galatians 3:13). The memorial supper commemorates the great hope that was generated for sinful man as Jesus was lifted up on the cross of Calvary to heal mankind. Let us lift our eyes and look to the cross for healing.

MEDITATION 20

Jesus, the Prophet Who Delivers

The Lord makes a powerful promise to Israel through Moses in Deuteronomy 18:18-19, "I will raise up for them a Prophet like you from among their brethren, and will put My words in His mouth, and He shall speak to them all that I command Him. And it shall be that whoever will not hear My words, which He speaks in My name, I will require it of him." Many have tried to identify this future prophet with various characters over time—Joshua, John the Baptist, Muhammad. Yet, the New Testament Scriptures make it clear this Prophet like Moses was Jesus Christ.

After Jesus multiplied loaves and fishes, those who had seen the sign declared, "This is truly the Prophet who is to come into the world" (John 6:14). Philip also declared to Nathanael, "We have found Him of whom Moses in the law...wrote—Jesus of Nazareth, the son of Joseph" (John 1:45). Peter quoted the Deuteronomy 18 passage as he proclaimed Jesus as the Prophet who would be like Moses (Acts 3:21-23). Stephen also quotes this passage as he declares Jesus to the stiff-necked Jewish council (Acts 7:37-38).

Various likenesses could be noted between Moses and Jesus. Both were born under an oppressive, foreign rule (Exodus 1:8-11; Luke 2:1-2). Both were threatened by a wicked king (Exodus 1:15-16; Matthew 2:16). Both were rejected by their own people (Exodus 32:1; Acts 7:37-39; Matthew 27:21-22; Acts 2:36). Both showed signs and wonders (Deuteronomy 34:10-12; John 5:36; Acts 2:22). Both made a covenant with blood (Exodus 24:7-8; Matthew 26:26-28).

Yet the most momentous miracle performed through Moses was the deliverance of the children of Israel out of the bondage of Egypt as they crossed the Red Sea on their way to the promised land. This deliverance is repetitively referred to in the Scriptures. Stephen said, "This Moses whom they rejected, saying, 'Who made you a ruler and a judge?' is the one God sent to be a ruler and a deliverer..." (Acts 7:35). Prior to this deliverance, Moses shed the blood of the Passover Lamb (Exodus 12-15). Similar to the Red Sea rescue, Jesus delivers us from the bondage of our sin as we are baptized into Him (Romans 6:3-6). Yet, baptism would have very little meaning if it were not for the blood our Passover Lamb of God shed for our sins on the cross. Because of His death, burial and resurrection we now can be delivered from death into a new life with Him.

God was foreshadowing our spiritual journey with Jesus in the events of the children of Israel long before Jesus walked this earth. The deliverance Moses provided Israel was but a faint shadow of the deliverance the Prophet like Moses would provide for all people centuries later. As we eat and drink from the elements celebrating our deliverance, let us give thanks that God sent Jesus, the Prophet like Moses. This Jesus was sent into the world to deliver us from the captivity of our sins and to lead us into a promised land of abundance, peace and rest. Praise God for our Deliverer.

MEDITATION 21

The Savior Who Leads to the Promised Land

The book of Joshua begins with the following words of encouragement from the Lord to Joshua after Moses has died:

> "Moses My servant is dead. Now therefore, arise, go over this Jordan, you and all this people, to the land which I am giving to them—the children of Israel. Every place that the sole of your foot will tread upon I have given you, as I said to Moses" (Joshua 1:2-3).

What a powerful moment! Finally, God's special nation can leave its wilderness sojourn and enter into the promised land led by their new leader, Joshua. While this is a momentous turning point in Biblical history, it is much more than a historical note.

As we look at this Old Testament story of the savior of Israel, Joshua, is it not beautiful to think God was painting a prophetic picture of the future Savior of the world, Jesus Christ? Just notice the glaring similarities.

- The name Joshua in Hebrew is the same name as Jesus in first century Greek and means "Jehovah saves" (Matthew 1:21).

- Joshua was preceded by a great leader, Moses, while Jesus was preceded by a great prophet, John (Joshua 1:1; John 3:15-17).

- Joshua led Israel after 40 years of wilderness wandering, just as Jesus leads all people out of our wandering lives of sin (Luke 15:3-6).

- God magnified Joshua by the Jordan River miracle and testified about His Son at His baptism in the Jordan (Matthew 3:13-17; John 1:29-33).

- Joshua set up twelve stones so Israel might remember God's saving power, and Jesus sent out twelve apostles to share His message with the world.

- Joshua gave Israel rest from their enemies temporarily, but Jesus offers rest from our greatest enemy for eternity (cp. Hebrews 4:8-9; Matthew 11:28-30).

As we compare the lives of Joshua and Jesus, we realize God was foreshadowing a greater Savior than Joshua—Jesus Christ. These comparisons are far more than mere coincidences. The Hebrew writer points out God was prefiguring a greater rest for the people of God than what was given in the days of Joshua (Hebrews 4:8-9).

Some argue there is nothing in a name, but there was certainly something in the names of Joshua and Jesus. It was a clue. It was a divine connection to an eternal plot. It was a revelation that the greater Joshua, the greater Savior, had been born. This fact is what the angel revealed when Joseph was first informed that Mary was carrying the Christ. The angel said, "And she will bring forth a Son, and you shall call His name JESUS, for He will save His people from their sins" (Matthew 1:21). Praise God our Savior has come to finally lead us home.

MEDITATION 22

Jesus Rescues His People

A sad cycle of a dark age begins in the days of the judges of Israel, just after the death of Joshua. Judges 2:11 summarizes the sad condition stating, "Then the children of Israel did evil in the sight of the Lord, and served the Baals..." As a result of Israel's sin, "...the anger of the Lord was hot against Israel. So He delivered them into the hands of plunderers who despoiled them; and He sold them into the hands of their enemies all around, so that they could no longer stand before their enemies. Wherever they went out, the hand of the Lord was against them for calamity, as the Lord had said, and as the Lord had sworn to them. And they were greatly distressed" (Judges 2:14-15).

God has always granted man free will, even if it means choosing evil. Yet, free will is also connected to consequences. Choosing evil will have negative spiritual results. Even so, in Judges, there is a message of hope. Israel rebelled, but the Lord always stayed close enough to hear their cries for mercy. Eventually,

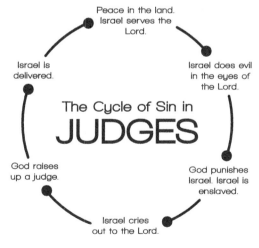

after the oppression was unbearable, the nation of Israel would remember they truly did need God and would seek His help. So, in response to their pleas for mercy, "the Lord raised up judges who delivered them out of the hand of those who plundered them" (2:16).

It must have been a wonderful thing to be delivered and rescued when all seemed hopeless. The people of Israel who remembered their plight must have fondly admired their God-sent deliverers who gave them peace and safety. Yet, in the cycle of the judges, soon they would forget and go right back to their sinful ways and suffer their miserable consequences again until God sent another deliverer to their rescue.

The memorial supper we share on a weekly basis is intended to prompt us to remember our Rescuer. We commune together in remembrance of our ultimate deliverer, Jesus Christ (1 Corinthians 11:24-25). In Paul's opening remarks to Galatia, Paul writes, "Grace to you and peace from God the Father and our Lord Jesus Christ, who gave Himself for our sins, that He might deliver us from this present evil age, according to the will of our God and Father, to whom be glory forever and ever. Amen" (Galatians 1:3-5, NKJV).

Maybe you have been delivered from a difficult situation—a dangerous encounter, a financial difficulty, or a life-threatening illness. The joy of being rescued stimulates an overwhelming feeling of gratitude toward those who rescue us. How great should our thanks be for Jesus? He has rescued us from the eternal consequences of our rebellion when He gave Himself for our sins. May the fond memory of our rescue from sin constantly be on our minds when Satan tries to bring us back into his grip again.

MEDITATION 23

Defeating the Enemy in Death

One of the deliverers of Israel in the days of the judges was Samson. Overall, Samson's character is far from being like Christ. Samson was rash, sensual, impulsive and overconfident. Yet, the shadows of Christ are never exact replicas. If they were, we would not need Jesus. Whether it be Adam, Noah, Abraham or Moses there were always flaws in the Old Testament examples of faith. Yet there are also faint shadows in these imperfect men of the perfect Jesus who would come to redeem and save man.

With Samson, we see a picture of the Savior to come in his final act. At this point in Samson's life, all seems hopeless. Delilah has unraveled gullible Samson's miraculous strength through her manipulation and deception (Judges 16:4-20). The Lord has departed from Samson to the point that Samson's enemies, the Philistines, have taken him as a trophy slave and put out his eyes (Judges 16:21-27). Yet, in one final, sacrificial act of strength, Samson asks for God to grant him the ability to deliver Israel from the hands of their enemy one final time. Judges 16:28-30 details Samson's final moments:

> "Then Samson called to the Lord, saying, 'O Lord God, remember me, I pray! Strengthen me, I pray, just this once, O God, that I may with one blow take vengeance on the Philistines for my two eyes!' And Samson took hold of the two middle pillars which supported the temple, and he braced himself against them, one on his right and the other on his left. Then Samson said, 'Let me die with the Philistines!'

And he pushed with all his might, and the temple fell on the lords and all the people who were in it. So the dead that he killed at his death were more than he had killed in his life."

The final result of Samson's death ought to resonate as we contemplate the life and death of Jesus. Jesus taught and touched multitudes of people during His life and ministry. Yet by His sacrificial death, our Lord destroyed Satan's power over us and has given the opportunity to billions of people through the ages of time to be saved through Him. 1 John 3:5, 8 says,

"And you know that He was manifested to take away our sins, and in Him there is no sin...He who sins is of the devil, for the devil has sinned from the beginning. For this purpose the Son of God was manifested, that He might destroy the works of the devil."

The havoc the devil has wreaked is far worse than any havoc the Philistines caused to Israel. Yet thankfully, the Savior God sent to the world to defeat the devil is far greater than fallible Samson too. Our Savior is the sinless Son of God Himself who came to destroy our enemy. Each Lord's Day, we memorialize His final act on the cross—His great sacrifice for our sins!

MEDITATION 24

The Kinsman Who Became Our Redeemer

The book of Ruth is a favorite for many Bible readers. Though the book is named after Ruth, it may just as easily be named for Boaz. Boaz is a pivotal character in the final three chapters of the work. Without Boaz's providential kindness, the lives of the helpless widows, Ruth and Naomi, may never be changed for the better. Boaz was the near kinsman who took Ruth as his wife and redeemed the land of Naomi's husband, Elimelech, as required in the law of Moses (see Leviticus 25:23-34; Deuteronomy 25:5-10).

Yet, perhaps, the most beautiful aspect of this book is how Boaz paints for us a faint picture of our Kinsman-Redeemer, Jesus Christ. One of the final comments recorded in Ruth is found in 4:14, "Blessed be the Lord, who has not left you this day without a close relative; and may his name be famous in Israel!" Indeed, as children of God, we are also blessed by a child, Jesus Christ. Galatians 4:4-7 says,

> "...when the fullness of the time had come, God sent forth His Son, born of a woman, born under the law, to redeem those who were under the law, that we might receive the adoption as sons. And because you are sons, God has sent forth the Spirit of His Son into your hearts, crying out, 'Abba, Father!' Therefore you are no longer a slave but a son, and if a son, then an heir of God through Christ."

In Boaz, Ruth and Naomi received an elevation in relationship. In Christ, we are no longer slaves but redeemed as sons. While our journey is interesting to contemplate, the one who changed the course of our destination is worthy of far greater contemplation. Thus, as we read Ruth, we think not just of the great character lessons we might learn from Ruth and Naomi but more so of the one who had the power to change their story. Should it not also be the same with us? Who deserves the greater focus—the redeemed son or the Redeemer, the Son of God? To further deepen this connection, consider seven similarities between Boaz and Jesus:

- Both are lord of the field and harvest (Ruth 2:2-3; Matthew 9:38; 1 Corinthians 3:9).

- Both were near kinsman, relatives (Ruth 2:3, 20; 4:14; Hebrews 2:14-15).

- Both were willing to supply the needs of others (Ruth 2:14-17; John 6:48-51).

- Both paid a purchase price for the redemption of others (Ruth 4:9; 1 Peter 1:18-19).

- Both gave rest to those who were weary (Ruth 3:1; Matthew 11:28-30).

- Both offer an inheritance to the redeemed (Ruth 4:10; Ephesians 1:7-21).

- Both make a covenant as a bridegroom (Ruth 4:13; John 3:29; Ephesians 5:25-27).

As we read of this beautiful love story, we gush at the idea of Boaz taking the time to notice a widowed, Moabite woman gleaning from his field. As we contemplate the sacrifice of Jesus, may we also celebrate the love of our Redeemer who died to save lost sinners who would be hopeless without His grace.

MEDITATION 25

Jesus, a King Greater Than David

The Lord made a powerful covenant with David's descendants through the words of Nathan the prophet recorded in 2 Samuel 7:12-13, "When your days are fulfilled and you rest with your fathers, I will set up your seed after you, who will come from your body, and I will establish his kingdom. He shall build a house for My name, and I will establish the throne of his kingdom forever" (see also verse 16).

The words of this powerful promise predict a king greater than David who would arise after David's death. He was greater because David's reign on the throne was only temporal. David was replaced by Solomon and for decades the kingly throne in Israel had a revolving door after every kingly death. As we read through the books of Kings and Chronicles, we never find a king whose throne was permanent. Almost always, the end of a king's reign is noted by their death.

However, as we turn into the pages of our New Testament, we are introduced to a descendant of David. The way Matthew phrases it immediately reminds us of the prophecy of 2 Samuel 7. He writes of the "genealogy of Jesus Christ, the Son of David..." (Matthew 1:1). Could it be, after these centuries, a descendant of David would finally rule on David's throne forever?

According to the angel who spoke to Mary at her conception, her child would "be called Son of the Highest; and the Lord God will give Him the throne of His father David. And He will reign over the house of Jacob forever, and of His kingdom there will be no end" (Luke 1:31-33). At the birth of Jesus, the wise men from the East inquired, "Where is He who has been born King of the Jews?" (Matthew 2:1-2). As Jesus journeyed into Jerusalem, multitudes of people cried out, "Hosanna! Blessed is He who comes in the name of the Lord! The King of Israel!" (John 12:13). Jesus Himself told Pilate, "You say rightly that I am a king. For this cause I was born, and for this cause I have come into the world..." (18:37).

Clearly, the Bible pronounces Jesus as king but how could He be a king forever? After the death, burial, and resurrection of Jesus, Peter declares the kingship of Jesus. He makes a simple point of comparison between David and Jesus, saying, "Men and brethren, let me speak freely to you of the patriarch David, that he is both dead and buried, and his tomb is with us to this day. Therefore, being a prophet, and knowing that God had sworn with an oath to him that of the fruit of his body, according to the flesh, He would raise up the Christ to sit on his throne, he, foreseeing this, spoke concerning the resurrection of the Christ, that His soul was not left in Hades, nor did His flesh see corruption. This Jesus God has raised up, of which we are all witnesses" (Acts 2:29-32).

David died. Jesus arose. For this reason, He has the power to reign forever. As members of the Lord's house, let us honor and glorify the King greater than David who came to earth to die for our sins and now reigns in the heavens.

MEDITATION 26

Jesus, a King Greater Than Solomon

The dreamy prayer of the incoming king Solomon in 1 Kings 3 is one of his most memorable moments. Though he could ask for anything, he asked for an understanding heart (1 Kings 3:9). From that point forward, Solomon is known for his wisdom (cp. 1 Kings 4:32). Yet, God grants to Solomon far more than just wisdom.

> "The speech pleased the Lord, that Solomon had asked this thing. Then God said to him: 'Because you have asked this thing, and have not asked long life for yourself, nor have asked riches for yourself, nor have asked the life of your enemies, but have asked for yourself understanding to discern justice, behold, I have done according to your words; see, I have given you a wise and understanding heart, so that there has not been anyone like you before you, nor shall any like you arise after you. And I have also given you what you have not asked: both riches and honor, so that there shall not be anyone like you among the kings all your days" (1 Kings 3:10-13).

Solomon's wisdom and glory was seen in various ways, but the immense, gaudy, gold-plated temple was perhaps the most impressive display eliciting worldwide architectural marvel. However, despite the greatness of Solomon, Jesus makes a daunting statement in Matthew 12:42 when He said, "indeed a greater than Solomon is here."

Several parallels help us pinpoint how Jesus was indeed greater than the greatest of all the Israelite kings. He was greater in wisdom since Christ is the wisdom of God (1 Corinthians 1:24). He was greater in riches, for

Solomon's were merely temporary, whereas Jesus gives us the riches of His grace which give us an eternal inheritance (Ephesians 1:7-14). Jesus was greater in honor, as the Lamb who was slain is worthy "to receive power and riches and wisdom, and strength and honor, and glory, and blessing!" (Revelation 5:12).

Perhaps the most vital comparison we may make is how Jesus was greater in His temple. Solomon's temple was a massive building project. The money for its building and architectural blueprints were all set up by Solomon's father, David (2 Samuel 7:11-16). Even so, a few centuries later, Solomon's temple was torn down. Conversely, Jesus once declared His trademark miracle was the raising up of His temple. In John 2:19 Jesus said, "Destroy this temple, and in three days I will raise it up." John remarks, "He was speaking of the temple of His body. Therefore, when He had risen from the dead, His disciples remembered that He had said this to them..." (John 2:21-22).

When Solomon died, he was buried in the City of David (1 Kings 11:43). At that point, his riches, glory, and honor were all relics of the past. When Jesus died, He rose again and still reigns in immortality. Therefore, He is worthy of all riches, honor and glory. He is a greater King than Solomon and His temple still stands with each Christian as living stones (1 Corinthians 3:9-11, 16-17; Ephesians 2:19-22; 1 Peter 2:4-5). Thus, we remember Him, above any other king, on this Lord's Day.

MEDITATION 27

Jesus, a Prophet Greater Than John the Baptist

In the Old Testament we read of two well-known prophets, Elijah and Elisha. Both were revered men in Israelite history. Interestingly, Jesus compares himself to both in Luke 4:24-27. While there may be points of similarity between Jesus and both prophets, there is an interesting difference in the ministries of Elijah and Elisha—namely that Elisha is granted a "double portion" of power. Interestingly, the Scriptures tell of many more miracles wrought by the hand of Elisha than Elijah. We see his greater ministry foreshadowed in 2 Kings 2:7-9 when Elijah passes the torch to his student, Elisha.

> "…the two of them stood by the Jordan. Now Elijah took his mantle, rolled it up, and struck the water; and it was divided this way and that, so that the two of them crossed over on dry ground. And so it was, when they had crossed over, that Elijah said to Elisha, 'Ask! What may I do for you, before I am taken away from you?' Elisha said, 'Please let a double portion of your spirit be upon me.'"

If we were to remove the names Elijah and Elisha from this text, then the events portrayed may sound quite similar to other passages in the New Testament. In the gospels we read of two men, John and Jesus, also standing in the waters of the river Jordan. John had prepared the way for Jesus and was known as a great prophet in his own right (see Luke 7:24-28). Yet, at the baptism of Jesus the torch is passed to one who John himself admits would deserve greater honor. Like Elisha following Elijah, the text of John 1:26-30 speaks of a greater prophet to follow John.

"John answered them, saying, 'I baptize with water, but there stands One among you whom you do not know. It is He who, coming after me, is preferred before me, whose sandal strap I am not worthy to loose.' These things were done in Bethabara beyond the Jordan, where John was baptizing. The next day John saw Jesus coming toward him, and said, 'Behold! The Lamb of God who takes away the sin of the world! This is He of whom I said, 'After me comes a Man who is preferred before me, for He was before me.'"

Pages and pages could be written as we compare and contrast the prophets Elijah and Elisha to John and Jesus. Yet, as we gather around the Lord's Table, we ought to remember the simple point John made about Jesus. Jesus is greater than Elijah. Jesus is greater than Elisha. Jesus is greater than John because Jesus is "the Lamb of God who takes away the sin of the world!" (John 1:29). None of these great prophets' blood would atone for the sins of the world except Jesus. None of their ministries were as far-reaching as the ministry of Jesus Christ. None of them existed prior to the foundation of the world except for the Son of God. For this reason, God separates Jesus from the rest of the prophetic pack in the waters of the Jordan when He says, "This is My beloved Son, in whom I am well pleased" (Matthew 3:17). May we also be well pleased to honor our Lord and Savior.

MEDITATION 28

The Greater Glory of the Temple

In 586 B.C. Nebuchadnezzar destroyed Solomon's temple. It was a moment of national sorrow and humiliation for the Jewish people. Yet, after seventy years of Babylonian captivity, King Cyrus of Persia allows the Jewish people to return to their homeland and rebuild their temple. Upon their return, God sends the prophet Haggai to motivate the procrastinating people of their task, saying, "Is it time for you yourselves to dwell in your paneled houses, and this temple to lie in ruins?" (Haggai 1:4).

So, the people do rebuild. Yet, the rebuilt temple was not nearly as wonderful as Solomon's temple the older generation remembered. Haggai writes, "Who is left among you who saw this temple in its former glory? And how do you see it now? In comparison with it, is this not in your eyes as nothing?" (Haggai 2:3). Even so, the Lord makes an interesting promise through Haggai. He says, "'The glory of this latter temple shall be greater than the former,' says the Lord of hosts. 'And in this place I will give peace'" (2:9).

Without Jesus, this statement just does not make much sense. After all, before Jesus, the temple would never match the epic beauty it reached in the days of Solomon. Furthermore, the people of God were never really at peace as they lived under the subjugation of foreign governments throughout the days of the Persians, Greeks, and Romans. So, in what way would the glory of the latter temple be greater than the former?

John may give us a clue. In the time of Christ the Jews asked, "'What sign do You show to us, since You do these things?' Jesus answered and said to them, 'Destroy this temple, and in three days I will raise it up'" (John 2:18-19). When Jesus made this statement, the Jews were clearly confused. They misunderstood what Jesus was referring to when He spoke of the temple just as we may also confuse Haggai's latter temple. The text continues, "Then the Jews said, 'It has taken forty-six years to build this temple, and will You raise it up in three days?' But He was speaking of the temple of His body."

When Jesus died, His temple being destroyed, there was a feeling of gloom among His disciples. Yet His body did not lie in ruins forever. Jesus rose from the dead a victor over the grave. God had glorified His Son by raising Him from the dead and exalted Him by placing Him on the throne. Through the sacrifice of Jesus, lost sinners could finally be at peace with God. His rebuilt temple is the basis of our hope. God's promise through Haggai was fulfilled. Because of the risen temple of His body, we can become the temple of God (1 Corinthians 3:16-17). This temple of God's people is not a temporary structure, subject to destruction. It is a people who are guaranteed by the very promise of the risen Savior Himself of future victory and everlasting glory in God's kingdom. For this reason, we celebrate the death, burial, and resurrection of Jesus—the earnest of our inheritance in the glorious kingdom of heaven God has prepared for His children. How glorious!

MEDITATION 29

Jesus, Suffering Before the Crown

Matthew 27:45-46 is a short excerpt from the crucifixion scene of Jesus containing one of the seven sayings of Jesus from the cross. Verse 45 indicates "from the sixth hour until the ninth hour there was darkness over all the land." Just prior to the death of Jesus, "about the ninth hour Jesus cried out with a loud voice, saying, 'Eli, Eli, lama sabachthani?' that is, 'My God, My God, why have You forsaken Me?'" (Matthew 27:46). If we only looked at the gospel account, our interpretation of this expression from Jesus may widely vary. Yet, to fully understand this statement, we must realize these words are not original to Him. Jesus, the Son of David, was quoting from the psalmist David.

David writes, "My God, My God, why have You forsaken Me? Why are You so far from helping Me, and from the words of My groaning? O My God, I cry in the daytime, but You do not hear; And in the night season, and am not silent" (Psalm 22:1-2).

Think of how David must have felt before he was crowned as king. His best friend, Jonathan, had to separate from him. The reigning king of Israel, Saul, envied and hated him. He fled from Saul's head-hunters and feared for his life. God had promised to anoint David to the throne, but in those moments, he felt forsaken and alone. Ultimately, we know the end of the story for David. Saul is defeated. David reigned upon his throne until his death. His reign, though marred by sadness and disappointments, is one of ultimate success and victory for the nation (which is foreshadowed in Psalm 22:21).

Fast forward to Jesus, the Son of David, on the cross. His story sounds eerily familiar. He has been unjustly attacked by His enemies. He has been betrayed, denied, and deserted by His disciples (Matthew 26:56). God had promised to exalt Him but here He was being mocked and humiliated on a cross. Feeling all of the pains and sorrows of humanity, it was easy to feel alone. Thus, Jesus fully could identify with and find comfort in David's 22nd Psalm. Psalm 22 is historic as it points us to David's life, but Messianic as it foreshadows the sufferings of the Messiah. Yet, greater than David's temporal throne, Jesus would be raised three days after these words. He would ascend on high and there He would be exalted to an eternal throne after defeating the greatest of all enemies—death. God had not abandoned His Son. The Father allowed the Son to suffer so He could give Him the victory crown.

In our lives, we may have moments where we feel alone, deserted, and abandoned. We may have moments where we question God's purposes as we are called to suffer despite living a life of faithful service. When those moments arise, it is good for us to go back to the cross and remember Jesus. He faced moments of tribulation. Yet He promises "be of good cheer, I have overcome the world" (John 16:33). Through His blood, we can overcome too. Let us not despair in the moments of darkness. Jesus, the Light, has arisen from the dead, giving hope when all seems hopeless.

MEDITATION 30

Jesus, the Reproach of Men Saves Men

Psalm 22 has been called "the psalm of the cross." One who is familiar with the gospel accounts of Jesus on the cross cannot help but notice the prophecies of David being played out in the life of Jesus. For example, in Psalm 22:6-8, David writes, "…I am a worm, and no man; a reproach of men, and despised by the people. All those who see Me ridicule Me; they shoot out the lip, they shake the head, saying, 'He trusted in the Lord, let Him rescue Him; let Him deliver Him, since He delights in Him!'"

Now notice the text in Matthew 27:39-44, "And those who passed by blasphemed Him, wagging their heads and saying, 'You who destroy the temple and build it in three days, save Yourself! If You are the Son of God, come down from the cross.' Likewise the chief priests also, mocking with the scribes and elders, said, 'He saved others; Himself He cannot save. If He is the King of Israel, let Him now come down from the cross, and we will believe Him. He trusted in God; let Him deliver Him now if He will have Him; for He said, "I am the Son of God."' Even the robbers who were crucified with Him reviled Him with the same thing."

Just a cursory reading of these two texts will help us to see several small details prophesied by David fulfilled in Jesus Christ hundreds of years later.

- Jesus was the reproach of men as seen by the people who blasphemed Him (Psalm 22:6; Matthew 27:39).

- Jesus was ridiculed by the people in statements such as, "You who destroy the temple and build it in three days, save Yourself," (Psalm 22:7; Matthew 27:40).

- The mockers were visibly seen wagging their heads in their disgust towards Jesus (Psalm 22:7; Matthew 27:40).

- Even the specific verbal attacks of His persecutors are paraphrased correctly as "He trusted in the Lord, let Him rescue Him," (Psalm 22:8; Matthew 27:43).

The precise predictive prophecies of David as we get into the details of the crucifixion of Jesus are an example of God's divine engineering. Yet, the irony of their attacks is also noteworthy. The passers-by, the priests, and even the petty criminals all mock Jesus with one common jeer: "Save Yourself!" No, Jesus did not save Himself from death. However, the refusal of Jesus to listen to their reproach ought to be cause for our grateful rejoicing. He died to save someone far more reproachable—guilty sinners like you and me. The reproach of men died to save reproachable men. May we rejoice that Jesus never came down from the cross when He was dared to do so. If He had been rescued from the cross, we would still be without hope.

MEDITATION 31

Jesus, Born to Die

One of our most vulnerable periods of life is when we are entirely at the mercy of others. The unborn child is completely dependent upon the health of the mother to live and thrive in the womb. From childbirth, the infant is completely dependent upon the nurturing and feeding of others. Without parents and caregivers, children's lives are at risk. In Psalm 22:9-11 the psalmist takes a moment to reflect on God's providence during these moments of vulnerability. David writes,

> "Yet you are he who took me from the womb; you made me trust you at my mother's breasts. On you was I cast from my birth, and from my mother's womb you have been my God. Be not far from me, for trouble is near, and there is none to help."

The context of the Messianic Psalm 22 looks ahead to Jesus Christ's helplessness on the cross. Upon the cross, Jesus was alone and vulnerable. No one would help Him. Not even God would allow His Son to come down off the cross. His own mother must helplessly watch from afar (Matthew 27:55-56).

This humiliation upon the cross is a stark contrast to the birth and infancy of Jesus where God's tender presence is constantly observed. The angel Gabriel announced the very conception of Jesus (Luke 1:26-38). Jesus is born in the small town of Bethlehem with His first crib as a meager manger. Yet, shepherds come to honor Him after a birth announcement delivered by angels stating "...there is born to you this day...a Savior, who is Christ the Lord" (Luke 2:1-18). Upon the first trip of Jesus to Jerusalem, two aged servants, Simeon and Anna, are overjoyed to finally meet the Christ (Luke 2:21-38). Later, jealous Herod orders the killing of all male children in Bethlehem but God protects Jesus by warning his parents they should take him to Egypt until it is safe to return (Matthew 2:2-18). Jesus grows up in poverty in Nazareth but is still growing in wisdom, and stature, and in favor with God and men all along (Luke 2:52). For a poor carpenter's son Jesus, was truly blessed as an infant and as a child.

However, despite God's providence and protection at birth, the somber reality for Jesus was that He was born to die. There would be a day when God would no longer protect His Son. There would be a time when His friends forsook Him. When His hour had come, Jesus knew He must refuse to call the angels to His aid. Most shockingly, the Father would allow the suffering and death of His Son without divine intervention. Why? Well, the answer to that question is why the birth of Jesus can be called "good news." Jesus died because He is our Savior and only through His punishment could He save His people from their sins (Matthew 1:21). As we come to reflect at the Lord's Table, we come remembering a child who, ironically, was born to die so that we might live. We ought to come with gratefulness to our God who allowed such suffering for our sakes.

MEDITATION 32

Jesus, Surrounded by Enemies

Every July since the 14th century, the city of Pamplona, Spain has held an interesting tradition—the running of the bulls. Full-grown bulls are released to run through the streets while people from all over the world, voluntarily, try to run away and avoid being gored or trampled. Each year, multiple people are injured, either from being gored by the bulls or after being trampled by one another.

A fierce, charging bull is a scary sight. Nobody wants to be voluntarily left in the street alone with a bull lunging at him. Likewise, nobody would want to be left alone in the circus ring with a raging and hungry lion.

Interestingly, the Messiah is pictured in Psalm 22 as being surrounded by both bulls and lions. Psalm 22:12-13 says, "Many bulls have surrounded Me; Strong bulls of Bashan have encircled Me. They gape at Me with their mouths, like a raging and roaring lion." As we scan the life of Jesus in the gospels, we never see any encounters with literal bulls or literal lions though. Instead, this was figurative language used to describe the bloodthirsty enemies of Jesus. Over and over in the gospels, the Pharisees, Sadducees, chief priests, and scribes are all described as rabidly hunting Jesus.

John 19:6-7 is one such instance: "Therefore, when the chief priests and officers saw Him, they cried out, saying, 'Crucify Him, crucify Him!' Pilate said to them, 'You take Him and crucify Him, for I find no fault in Him.' The Jews answered him, 'We have a law, and according to our law He ought to die, because He made Himself the Son of God.'"

Undeservedly, Jesus became a hunted man when He walked this earth. His greatest enemies used one of His disciples to betray Him and entrap Him. In His final hours, He was surrounded by enemies who shouted for His crucifixion. Yet, Jesus did not run from the assault. He voluntarily listened to their misleading accusations, subjected Himself to their unlawful trial, and went to the cross without a word. He was the Lamb of God surrounded by the lions. Yet, He allowed the bloodthirsty to spill His blood because it was the ransom price for our sins. He was pierced, gored, and mutilated not because He deserved it but because we did—and He took the pain so God would show mercy on us.

As we gather around the Lord's table today, let's remember the Lord who was surrounded by enemies—but still stood. As the hymn "Man of Sorrows" proclaims,

> "Bearing shame and scoffing rude,
> In my place condemned He stood;
> Sealed my pardon with His blood;
> Hallelujah! what a Savior!"

MEDITATION 33

His Blood Flowed for Us

Imagine the loss of blood Jesus must have experienced on the cross. He is struck on the face and may have begun to bleed from his mouth, nose or cheeks as the result. He is whipped and scourged so his entire back would have been cut open from the glass and bone which was often woven into the leather whip. A crown of thorns was placed on his head, most likely piercing through his scalp as it was pressed down. As He is crucified, his wrists, and possibly his feet, are pierced through with nails.

To stay alive, Jesus would have to press His bloodied back against the cross and push up with all of His strength to allow Himself to take a quick breath through the excruciating pain (the word "excruciating" is made, purposefully, from the word "crucify"). The Nazarene would have been dehydrated, exhausted and completely humiliated. He would have felt like this:

> "I am poured out like water,
> And all My bones are out of joint;
> My heart is like wax;
> It has melted within Me.
> My strength is dried up like a potsherd,
> And My tongue clings to My jaws;
> You have brought Me to the dust of death."
> (Psalm 22:14-15)

The phrase "poured out like water" is an accurate description of how the cross would have made Jesus feel. Spill water onto the soil outside and it becomes useless to us. It has been spent and wasted. Jesus, on the cross, was spent. Notice some of the verbs in this passage: "poured out, melted, dried up." All of them describe the withering of Jesus in His humanity.

71

Yet, the suffering of Jesus on the cross was all for a greater purpose. It accomplished something for us. John writes, "After this, Jesus, knowing that all things were now accomplished, that the Scripture might be fulfilled, said, 'I thirst!' Now a vessel full of sour wine was sitting there; and they filled a sponge with sour wine, put it on hyssop, and put it to His mouth" (John 19:28-29). On the cross, the sweat and blood of Jesus flowed until He was "poured out like water." This loss of bodily fluids caused His mouth to become painfully dry and He cried out, "I thirst!" Yet He emptied Himself so we might be filled up. He thirsted so our spiritual thirst might be quenched in Him. His blood flowed to accomplish, for us, a redemption to God we could never achieve without His sacrifice. May we never forget to give thanks to our Lord who suffered so intensely for our sins which put Him on the cross.

MEDITATION 34

Jesus, Pierced for Us

What happens to your belongings after you die? For those of us with children or grandchildren, they may inherit some of our most valuable possessions. Other possessions are often given away or just auctioned off. Most people usually wait until our loved ones have died to do anything with their belongings. It would be insulting to see them auctioning off our stuff as if we were dead already and they were already counting out their inheritance.

Yet, this is the situation Jesus finds Himself in on the cross. He is not even dead yet and the soldiers are casting lots for His clothing as He looks below from the cross. To those soldiers, it is only a matter of time before Jesus is a dead man and He will not be needing those clothes again.

Interestingly, the psalmist predicted this insulting scene centuries before it ever happened in the life of Jesus.

> "For dogs have surrounded Me; The congregation of the wicked has enclosed Me. They pierced My hands and My feet; I can count all My bones. They look and stare at Me. They divide My garments among them, And for My clothing they cast lots" (Psalm 22:16-18).

Luke records this actual event: "Then Jesus said, 'Father, forgive them, for they do not know what they do.' And they divided His garments and cast lots. And the people stood looking on. But even the rulers with them sneered, saying, "'He saved others; let Him save Himself if He is the Christ, the chosen of God'" (Luke 23:34-35).

The callous and cold attitude of those surrounding Jesus is alarming as we read through the text. The soldiers are just dividing up his clothes as if

Jesus is dead already. The people are, indeed, just staring at the Messiah as Psalm 22 predicted. The rulers are sneering and mocking Jesus for not saving Himself. Yet on the other end of the spectrum, the amazing love of Jesus would not shine so brightly without the darkness of these others on the scene. Just imagine hearing and seeing what Jesus saw while exposed on the cross and being able to say, "Father, forgive them, for they do not know what they do" (Luke 23:34). Thank God that Jesus did indeed offer forgiveness to sinners through His blood. Thank God He did not save Himself, for He stayed on the cross to save us.

As we remember our Lord, let's think on the one whose clothes were divided among sinners so sinners could be clothed with Christ.

MEDITATION 35

His Victory Is Our Victory

What do you think of when you hear the word "victory"? The mighty nation who fends off its foes and wins the war? The team who competes all season long and finally comes home with the championship? The survivor who battles cancer and overcomes the suffering involved in treatments to live a longer life? What about Jesus Christ Himself who suffered and died only to overcome the futile attempts of His enemies to silence the Son of God?

The ultimate portrait of Psalm 22 is a picture of the victory of Jesus. In the beginning, the outlook seems grim. It feels as though God has left the Son alone (Psalm 22:1). The moments the Savior faces seem so helplessly humiliating (Psalm 22:6-18). Yet God never forgot His Son. Though faced with the "dust of death," God delivered, saved, and answered the Son! Notice these exact terms used in Psalm 22:19-22:

> "...O Lord, do not be far from Me; O My Strength, hasten to help Me! Deliver Me from the sword, My precious life from the power of the dog. Save Me from the lion's mouth And from the horns of the wild oxen! You have answered Me. I will declare Your name to My brethren; In the midst of the assembly I will praise You."

Thankfully, the details of the Son overcoming death is not where this story ends. Because the Son is a victor, all those who are part of His holy nation, His team, His body can be overcomers too. We are confident of our own victory in the face of death because of His victory over death. This is the ultimate message of Paul in the resurrection chapter of 1 Corinthians 15.

> "So when this corruptible has put on incorruption, and this mortal has put on immortality, then shall be brought to pass the saying that

is written: 'Death is swallowed up in victory.' 'O Death, where is your sting? O Hades, where is your victory?' The sting of death is sin, and the strength of sin is the law. But thanks be to God, who gives us the victory through our Lord Jesus Christ" (1 Corinthians 15:54-57).

What should be our response to such a victory? In the real world, we celebrate heroes. We write books about victory. We throw parades when the victors come home. We openly praise those who rescue and deliver us from a hopeless situation. Likewise, as we gather around the Lord's Table, we are remembering but also celebrating. As the Psalmist wrote, "In the midst of the assembly I will praise You" (Psalm 22:22; see also Hebrews 2:12). So, the Supper we take is not done in private. It is done as we come together as a church (1 Corinthians 11:18) to celebrate together what the Lord has done for us, as His church, through His Son. We celebrate Jesus because His victory is our victory.

MEDITATION 36

Jesus, the Shepherd-King

Before David became the king who would replace Saul, he was just a shepherd boy from Bethlehem. 1 Samuel 17:15 says, "But David occasionally went and returned from Saul to feed his father's sheep at Bethlehem." This passage indicates David's loyalty to his father's sheep even when he was a royal musician for the king (1 Samuel 16:17-23).

Later in the text, David recalls his own courage and sacrifice in protecting his sheep from harm. As he is on the verge of confronting Goliath, he tells King Saul, "Your servant used to keep his father's sheep, and when a lion or a bear came and took a lamb out of the flock, I went out after it and struck it, and delivered the lamb from its mouth; and when it arose against me, I caught it by its beard, and struck and killed it" (1 Samuel 17:34-35). David's argument is that he was required to act courageously and take risks in the past and those moments prepared him for battle with Goliath on Israel's behalf (17:36).

The life that follows David's brave victory over Goliath takes a providential turn. He defeats Goliath (1 Samuel 17:48-50). His popularity grows with the people but arouses the jealousy of King Saul (18:7-9). Eventually, jealous Saul dies and David is crowned as the new king (1 Samuel 2:1-4). His kingship has its own trials and challenges but David is viewed as a successful king and "a man after God's own heart" (1 Samuel 13:14). This promotion from shepherd to king seems an unlikely leap. Yet, the work of shepherding prepared David for the work and sacrifices involved in shepherding God's special nation.

Like David, the New Testament speaks of another shepherd from Bethlehem: Jesus Christ. Jesus says, "I am the good shepherd. The good shepherd gives His life for the sheep" (John 10:11). Shepherding takes work. It takes courage. It may even require the ultimate sacrifice. Jesus was willing to do those things for His flock. Later, He would say, "I am the good shepherd; and I know My sheep, and am known by My own. As the Father knows Me, even so I know the Father; and I lay down My life for the sheep" (John 10:14-15).

Like David, Jesus came to do good and to help His people. Unfortunately, like David, Jesus had to battle with jealous enemies who sought to destroy Him in the midst of His earthly mission. Eventually, Jesus would literally die for the sheep. Yet after His death, He was raised and forever enthroned and pronounced as a Shepherd-King far greater than David (Acts 2:30-36).

Praise God we have a Good Shepherd who gives His life for the sheep. As the flock feed at the Lord's Table on the Lord's Day, we remember our Good Shepherd-King who courageously battled against God's enemies and won the victory over Satan for us. May we remember He shed His own blood so we could be one flock with one shepherd entering into His heavenly pastures through Him, the one door (John 10:9; cp. Psalm 23).

MEDITATION 37

Jesus, the Rejected Stone

There are two key Messianic prophecies that refer to the Messiah as a "cornerstone" (Psalm 118:22; Isaiah 28:16).

"The stone which the builders rejected
Has become the chief cornerstone.
This was the Lord's doing;
It is marvelous in our eyes."
(Psalm 118:22-23)

Jesus the Messiah and His apostles refer back to these passages several times in their speeches and writings (Matthew 21:33-44; Acts 4:10-12; Ephesians 2:20; 1 Peter 2:4-8).

The first time Jesus refers to Himself as the chief cornerstone is after His parable of the landowner in Matthew 21. In this parable, Jesus speaks of a landowner who owned a vineyard but leased it to vinedressers (Matthew 21:33). Unfortunately, those vinedressers began to think they were the owners, and whenever servants were sent to correct them, the servants were rejected and even killed. Finally, the landowner sent his son to them but those vinedressers even killed the son, too!

The interpretation of this parable is quite simple. The landowner is God who created the world. The Jews were the vinedressers who cared for His special nation, for a time, and were given special responsibilities to uphold. The servants were the prophets and messengers of God who often had a role in correcting God's leaders and those entrusted to lead Israel. Finally, Jesus is the Son whom they also killed. Jesus concludes this parable in Matthew 21:42-43 with the quotation of Psalm 118:22-23.

To a degree, Jesus was mixing his metaphors here. He jumps from the vineyard business to the construction business. However, He does so because the prophecy's fulfillment is a powerful conclusion to the parable's message. Jesus the Son was rejected. He was treated like a stone which the builders rejected when He was put onto a cross and treated like the trash heap of humanity. Yet, God rescued the Son. God saw fit to take that rejected stone and make Him the most important stone on a building.

The chief cornerstone of a building plays a vital role. It must be strong to hold the weight of the building. It must be square to keep the corners fitting together tightly. It is often chosen because of its beauty as well since it is placed at a visible location on the building. If the cornerstone is not in place, the rest of the structure of the building is compromised. What a beautiful picture of Jesus Christ! Rejected by men, but chosen by God and truly marvelous in our eyes. And, even more amazing, God prophesied it would all happen through the pens of His prophets hundreds of years before. Give glory to the God whose plan to redeem us has been in motion for centuries.

MEDITATION 38

Jesus, Too Important to Come Down

Nehemiah made an incredible sacrifice when he chose to leave his role as the king's cupbearer in the fortress city of Susa (Nehemiah 1:1, 11). While he could have enjoyed the comforts of the Persian palaces, he left to help rebuild the walls of the humbled and humiliated city of Jerusalem. His efforts did not come without criticism. Nehemiah 6:1-3 details a short excerpt of such mockery:

> "Now it happened when Sanballat, Tobiah, Geshem the Arab, and the rest of our enemies heard that I had rebuilt the wall, and that there were no breaks left in it (though at that time I had not hung the doors in the gates), that Sanballat and Geshem sent to me, saying, 'Come, let us meet together among the villages in the plain of Ono.' But they thought to do me harm.

> So I sent messengers to them, saying, 'I am doing a great work, so that I cannot come down. Why should the work cease while I leave it and go down to you?'"

There is an interesting comparison we could make to this episode in the rebuilding of Jerusalem's walls. Just as Nehemiah made a great sacrifice by leaving the palace to go to Jerusalem, Jesus made a great sacrifice by leaving heaven to come to sinful earth (Philippians 2:5-8). Just as Nehemiah accomplished what very few thought he could accomplish, Jesus also accomplished what He intended to do (John 19:30). Just as Nehemiah had his critics who wanted to stop his work on the wall, Jesus had critics who hoped to interrupt His work on the cross. Notice Mark's account of those who told Jesus to come down from the cross:

> "And those who passed by blasphemed Him, wagging their heads and saying, 'Aha! You who destroy the temple and build it in three days, save Yourself, and come down from the cross!'... And Jesus cried out with a loud voice, and breathed His last" (Mark 15:29-30, 37).

Nehemiah would not allow the critics of the wall to stop the work being accomplished. Jesus would not allow His critics on the cross to prevent the atoning sacrifice which was accomplished on that cross. Just as the wall was for the protection of the citizens of God's people in Jerusalem, the cross was for the protection of all those who are a part of the heavenly Jerusalem today (Hebrews 12:22). Only by the blood of Jesus Christ do we find the forgiveness of sins and protection from Satan's power (Ephesians 1:7). May our hearts be full of thankfulness for a Christ who gave up heaven so we might share eternity with Him.

MEDITATION 39

Jesus, the Sign of the Prophet Jonah

The character of Jonah is nowhere near a likeness of what we see in the personality of Jesus. Jonah is a rebellious pouter when it comes to God's mission to go preach to the Ninevites. Jesus was willingly obedient with regard to His mission on earth. Despite the dissimilarities, two key events in Jonah's preaching mission to Nineveh are highlighted by Jesus Himself as God-ordained pointers prefiguring the Christ.

The first has to do with Jonah's episode with the great fish noted in Jonah 1:17: "Now the Lord had prepared a great fish to swallow Jonah. And Jonah was in the belly of the fish three days and three nights." Jonah ended up in that great fish because he tried to run away from Nineveh when God told him to go to Nineveh (1:1). God still found a way to get him to Nineveh. He created a tempestuous storm which led to Jonah being thrown overboard and being swallowed by the fish. There, he was disgustingly protected for three days until the fish could vomit him onto the shores and he was sent, again, to Nineveh.

When Jonah arrives in Nineveh, a remarkable event occurs in the hearts of the people from that wicked and violent Gentile nation (read the prophet Nahum's message to Nineveh): they repent. Their repentance is the second key event Jesus mentions. Because of the preaching of Jonah, "the people of Nineveh believed God, proclaimed a fast, and put on sackcloth, from the greatest to the least of them" (Jonah 3:5). Because of their repentance, "God saw their works, that they turned from their evil way; and God relented from the disaster that He had said He would bring upon them, and He did not do it" (Jonah 3:10).

So, in what ways do these two events point us to Jesus? Let Jesus tell us: "...no sign will be given...except the sign of the prophet Jonah. For as Jonah was three days and three nights in the belly of the great fish, so will the Son of Man be three days and three nights in the heart of the earth. The men of Nineveh will rise up in the judgment with this generation and condemn it, because they repented at the preaching of Jonah; and indeed a greater than Jonah is here" (Matthew 12:39-41).

In Jesus, we see the sign of the prophet Jonah fulfilled. First, because like Jonah, Jesus spent three days in the heart of the earth after His death on the cross. Second, because like sinful Nineveh, after Jesus overcame the grave, His preaching led to the repentance and salvation of both Jews and Gentiles (Romans 1:16).

On the surface, Jonah may seem to be very little like Jesus. But, dig a little deeper, and the gospel story of the death, burial, and resurrection of Jesus is foreshadowed by that old prophet. Yet even better, the preaching which saves men is predetermined. Thanks be to God that salvation is not just for one ancient city but for all people, for all time. Thanks be to Jesus He voluntarily came to earth so we could be saved through Him.

MEDITATION 40

Jesus, Delivered Like Jeremiah

Jeremiah the prophet was called to prophesy during a dark time in Israel's history. The Jewish people were being besieged and on the verge of being taken captive by the Babylonians and Jeremiah was to give the final warning cries to a hard-hearted people who were too blind to change. Jeremiah's entire ministry was full of trials. It is no wonder he is called "the weeping prophet." In Jeremiah 38, we read of one particular instance where the leaders of Jerusalem are so tired of hearing Jeremiah they ask the king for permission to kill him (38:4). Instead, Jeremiah 38:6 says, "they took Jeremiah and cast him into the dungeon...and they let Jeremiah down with ropes. And in the dungeon there was no water, but mire. So Jeremiah sank in the mire."

Eventually, just as God promised, Jeremiah was pulled up out of the dungeon (Jeremiah 38:8-13; cp. 1:8, 19). Yet this episode had a lasting impact on Jeremiah. He references it in Lamentations 3:52-58: "My enemies without cause hunted me down like a bird. They silenced my life in the pit and threw stones at me. The waters flowed over my head; I said, 'I am cut off!' I called on Your name, O Lord, from the lowest pit. You have heard my voice: 'Do not hide Your ear from my sighing, from my cry for help.' You drew near on the day I called on You, and said, 'Do not fear!' O Lord, You have pleaded the case for my soul; You have redeemed my life."

There is no specific New Testament reference to this episode in Jeremiah's life. However, it is certainly reminiscent of the suffering our Lord faced. In fact, just like Jeremiah, Jesus knew the path of difficulty that lie ahead of

Him. Matthew 20:17-19 says, "Now Jesus, going up to Jerusalem, took the twelve disciples aside on the road and said to them, 'Behold, we are going up to Jerusalem, and the Son of Man will be betrayed to the chief priests and to the scribes; and they will condemn Him to death, and deliver Him to the Gentiles to mock and to scourge and to crucify. And the third day He will rise again.'"

Like Jeremiah, Jesus preached a message of repentance that was not well-received by many hearers. Like Jeremiah, Jesus was hated by the Jewish leaders who wanted to silence His message. Like Jeremiah, Jesus was cruelly punished by the Jewish rulers. And finally, like Jeremiah, Jesus was delivered from His enemies when the stone was removed from His tomb and He was raised up by God. Through Jeremiah, we see a faint foreshadowing of the suffering and deliverance our Lord would one day endure on our behalf. Because of Jesus, we can say, along with Jeremiah, "O Lord, You have pleaded the case for my soul; You have redeemed my life." May we remember His redemption as we gather around His table and set our minds on Him.

MEDITATION 41

Unto Us a Son Is Given

It is nearly universally conceded by Bible scholars that Isaiah 9:6-7 refers to the Messiah: "For unto us a Child is born, unto us a Son is given; and the government will be upon His shoulder. And His name will be called Wonderful, Counselor, Mighty God, Everlasting Father, Prince of Peace. Of the increase of His government and peace there will be no end, upon the throne of David and over His kingdom, to order it and establish it with judgment and justice from that time forward, even forever. The zeal of the Lord of hosts will perform this."

We could focus on the various appellations given to the Child who was to come, but instead we want to focus on only a couple of key terms in this passage as we prepare our minds for the Lord's Table.

Notice the phrase in verse 6, "Unto us a Son is given..." One of God's greatest gifts for all of mankind is His Son. John 3:16 says, "For God so loved the world that He gave His only begotten Son, that whoever believes in Him should not perish but have everlasting life." This gift God gave was not an unexpected one, but a promise the prophets foretold.

Yet one of the most beautiful aspects of this gift is what it truly offers to the hearts of those who allow the Son to reign in their lives. Isaiah 9:7 says, "Of the increase of His government and peace there will be no end..." The kingdom the Christ would establish would not provide a temporal peace that could be snuffed out as the kingdoms of this world rise and fall. Instead, the peace of Christ would endure from generation to generation. It was extended to all for as long as time exists.

The final phrase of Isaiah 9:7 says, "The zeal of the Lord of hosts will perform this." The gospel of Luke alludes to the accomplishment of these promises at the birth of Jesus.

> "And behold, you will conceive in your womb and bring forth a Son, and shall call His name Jesus. He will be great, and will be called the Son of the Highest; and the Lord God will give Him the throne of His father David. And He will reign over the house of Jacob forever, and of His kingdom there will be no end" (Luke 1:31-33).

What wonderful news Mary received! Her Son was the one Isaiah and so many more prophets and inspired men had spoken of long ago. Her Son would reign with all authority after His death, burial, and resurrection. Her Son would offer forgiveness of sins and peace to those forgiven through His shed blood. For this reason, at His birth the heavenly host could exclaim: "Glory to God in the highest, And on earth peace, goodwill toward men!" (Luke 2:14).

MEDITATION 42

Jesus, Marred for Us

I saiah 53 is an oft-quoted prophetic text because it so clearly alludes to the suffering of Jesus leading up to the cross. However, the thought of the Isaiah 53 text likely begins in chapter 52. Verses 13-15 say,

> "Behold, my servant shall act wisely; he shall be high and lifted up, and shall be exalted. As many were astonished at you—his appearance was so marred, beyond human semblance, and his form beyond that of the children of mankind—so shall he sprinkle many nations. Kings shall shut their mouths because of him, for that which has not been told them they see, and that which they have not heard they understand..." (52:13-15, ESV).

The previous time the phrase "Behold! My Servant" is used is in Isaiah 42:1. In fact, it is often used with reference to the chosen Servant of God (see Isaiah 42:1, 19; 43:10; 53:11). The Isaiah 42 passage specifically refers to one who would "bring justice to the Gentiles" (42:2). Yet in Isaiah 52, the thought turns to the Servant being lifted up and then exalted, but only after an astonishing event that would alter the very visage and form of the Servant.

In Matthew's account of the crucifixion of Jesus, he notes "they spat in His face and beat Him; and others struck Him with the palms of their hands, saying, 'Prophesy to us, Christ! Who is the one who struck You?'" (Matthew 26:67-68). Of course, being spit upon, beat and slapped would be enough to drastically alter one's appearance, just as Isaiah had prophesied in the 8th century B.C.

Furthermore, in the book of John, Jesus borrows some of the Jewish prophet's terminology, saying, "And I, if I am lifted up from the earth, will draw all peoples to Myself" (John 12:32). The reference is to Jesus being lifted up on a cross, drawing all nations, including Gentiles, which resulted in His ultimate exaltation to the throne and triumph over Satan (cp. Acts 2:23, 32-33).

Thus, the picture of God's Servant is a picture of triumph after tragedy, exaltation after embarrassment, victory after violence. It is this very picture which draws us to the Lord's Table with the realization the Servant endured all this suffering to serve us by dying for sins we committed. If this Servant does not refer to Jesus, then to whom does it refer? But, if it refers to Jesus, may we take this time to remember His sacrifice extolling the highest praise for our exalted and everlasting King.

MEDITATION 43

Jesus, the Rejected Man of Sorrows

Rejection can be an emotionally devastating occurrence. We feel sorry for the kid who gets picked last as his peers line up on the playground to pick teams. Our heart breaks for the teenager who has a crush and gets rejected on a date. More seriously, nothing may be worse than a child whose father has nothing to do with him or a spouse who is rejected by their mate for the short-lived joys of an affair. Rejection hurts.

With that thought in mind, imagine how Jesus felt as He had a front row seat to the ultimate rejection scene while being examined by Pontius Pilate, the Roman governor:

> "The governor answered and said to them, 'Which of the two do you want me to release to you?' They said, 'Barabbas!'
>
> Pilate said to them, 'What then shall I do with Jesus who is called Christ?'
>
> They all said to him, 'Let Him be crucified!'
>
> Then the governor said, 'Why, what evil has He done?'
>
> But they cried out all the more, saying, 'Let Him be crucified!'" (Matthew 27:21-23).

Jesus is rejected by His own countrymen in favor of a criminal. Barabbas, the common criminal, is released. Jesus, the King of kings, is condemned. It is hard to fathom why such poor choices can be made where the superior is rejected and the inferior is accepted. Yet, it happens. In fact, such rejection was predicted by Isaiah the prophet.

Isaiah writes, "...to whom has the arm of the Lord been revealed? For He shall grow up before Him as a tender plant, And as a root out of dry ground. He has no form or comeliness; And when we see Him, There is no beauty that we should desire Him. He is despised and rejected by men, A Man of sorrows and acquainted with grief. And we hid, as it were, our faces from Him; He was despised, and we did not esteem Him" (Isaiah 53:1-3).

An interesting contrast is made in this passage. It is a contrast of perspective. From God's perspective, Jesus would be like a tender plant (Isaiah 53:2). We care deeply for our plants as they begin to grow in their early days. We weed around them. We water them. We are hopeful they will bloom and produce for us. This is how God viewed Jesus.

Yet to others, Jesus was like a root out of dry ground (Isaiah 53:2). We care very little for a dried-up twig. We kick it out of our way. We step over top of it and think of it no more. To many, Jesus was like that root out of dry ground. He was rejected and cast aside. Yet, He willingly suffered the humiliation of rejection as a Man of sorrows for our sakes. And, it is His rejection that has led to our acceptance back into God's family. As we reflect on the cross, think upon the hurt Jesus endured because of the love He had for us.

MEDITATION 44

Jesus, by His Stripes We Are Healed

The thought of a suffering Messiah was a difficult concept to comprehend. Paul writes, "...the message of the cross is foolishness to those who are perishing, but to us who are being saved it is the power of God" (1 Corinthians 1:18). Later, he would write, "...we preach Christ crucified, to the Jews a stumbling block..." (1:23). The thought of a crucified Christ was a stumbling block to the Jews because they could not fathom an all-powerful God cruelly suffering punishment at the hands of men on a Roman cross.

If the suffering of Jesus were without purpose, perhaps we could sympathize with the common Jewish view. If Jesus never rose from the dead, we might also see His death as an ultimate defeat. Yet the purpose of Christ's suffering is clearly not due to his powerlessness, but for a propitiatory purpose—the atoning sacrifice for our sins.

> "Surely he has borne our griefs and carried our sorrows; yet we esteemed him stricken, smitten by God, and afflicted. But he was pierced for our transgressions; he was crushed for our iniquities; upon him was the chastisement that brought us peace, and with his wounds we are healed" (Isaiah 53:4-5).

Threads of Isaiah's work can be found within the writings of 1 Peter (a work with a heavy focus on suffering). This same message of purposeful and propitiatory suffering can be found in this segment of 1 Peter 2:

> "He committed no sin, neither was deceit found in his mouth. When he was reviled, he did not revile in return; when he suffered, he did

not threaten, but continued entrusting himself to him who judges justly. He himself bore our sins in his body on the tree, that we might die to sin and live to righteousness. By his wounds you have been healed. For you were straying like sheep, but have now returned to the Shepherd and Overseer of your souls" (1 Peter 2:22-25).

These passages help us realize something about the suffering of Jesus. It ought not be viewed as a picture of ugly and helpless defeat. It is the ultimate picture of redemption and victory for man. It is for our griefs, our sorrows, our transgressions, our iniquities and our sins. The purpose of His suffering was for our peace and our righteousness and our healing. This is the beauty of the cross.

There can be beauty in suffering if we just look for it. There is a beauty in the love a mother would show when she stays up all night suffering from sleeplessness to rock and care for her sick child. There is a beauty in the soldier who would take a bullet to suffer for his country's freedoms. There is beauty in the father who suffers while working three jobs to pay off his family's bills and to keep food on the table. Likewise, we need to see the beauty in a Christ who bore the cross for us. Let's not allow the cross to be a stumbling block but a stepping stone to a deeper appreciation of God's love for us.

MEDITATION 45

Jesus, Our Propitiation

Propitiation. It is a big word we do not use in ordinary, everyday conversation. It is a word found in John's epistle where He calls Jesus our propitiation. Notice the text, "My little children, these things I write to you, so that you may not sin. And if anyone sins, we have an Advocate with the Father, Jesus Christ the righteous. And He Himself is the propitiation for our sins, and not for ours only but also for the whole world" (1 John 2:1-2).

The term propitiation is defined as "an appeasing" (*Thayer's Greek Definitions*). The term appease in this definition may help us come closer to understanding how Jesus is our propitiation. To properly understand though, we must ask, "Whom was Jesus trying to appease?"

Other passages make it clear it is God who is appeased through the sacrifice of Jesus Christ. A walk through Romans can help us see how our sins affect our relationship with God and how the death of Jesus helped reverse it. Romans 1:18 says, "For the wrath of God is revealed from heaven against all ungodliness and unrighteousness of men, who by their unrighteousness suppress the truth." Romans 2:5 says, "But because of your hard and impenitent heart you are storing up wrath for yourself on the day of wrath when God's righteous judgment will be revealed." Later, the Romans text gives us a clue as to who can save us from God's wrath—Jesus. Romans 5:9 says, "Since, therefore, we have now been justified by his blood, much more shall we be saved by him from the wrath of God."

Thus, the concept of Jesus being a propitiation is the simple idea His death, for our sins, was a gift on our behalf to appease the wrath of God. To seal the idea, consider an illustration. A little child sins against his mother.

She is visibly upset and the child can sense her anger. Out of sorrow, the child goes out into the yard and plucks a few flowers and brings them into his mother. The flowers, of course, will die. Yet somehow, this gift is the propitiation which helps turn the mother's heart from a heart of disappointment into one of forgiveness.

Jesus is the beautiful flower who died to win God's heart back to His children. Therefore, as we read the prophetic words of Isaiah 53:6, we are filled with gratitude as we think of this great sacrificial gift Jesus offered so we might be won back to God.

> "All we like sheep have gone astray;
> We have turned, every one, to his own way;
> And the Lord has laid on Him the iniquity of us all."
> (Isaiah 53:6)

MEDITATION 46

Jesus, the Slaughtered Lamb of God

In Acts 8, we read of a Jewish proselyte from Ethiopia whose life was changed on his chariot ride from Jerusalem back into his native country. Several factors are involved in this life-changing moment. An angel of the Lord sends Philip to go preach to a man out in the desert (Acts 8:26). Philip goes and takes the time to ask, "Do you understand what you are reading?" (Acts 8:30). The Ethiopian himself was receptive to instruction and says, "How can I unless someone guides me?" (Acts 8:31). And, Philip takes the time to explain the text which was creating confusion in the mind of the eunuch (8:32-35). All of these factors—the angel, the preacher, the open-minded student, the teaching itself—are involved in the Ethiopian's confession, "I believe that Jesus Christ is the Son of God," and his subsequent baptism (8:35-39).

Yet what was the life-changing text which led the Ethiopian to this decision? Whom was this text referring to? The eternity-changing text for the Ethiopian was Isaiah 53, specifically verses seven and eight.

"He was oppressed and He was afflicted,
Yet He opened not His mouth;
He was led as a lamb to the slaughter,
And as a sheep before its shearers is silent,
So He opened not His mouth.

He was taken from prison and from judgment,
And who will declare His generation?
For He was cut off from the land of the living;
For the transgressions of My people He was stricken."

When Philip realizes the Ethiopian is struggling to understand the identity of Isaiah's prophecy, He immediately strives to help. The text in Acts 8 says,

> "So the eunuch answered Philip and said, 'I ask you, of whom does the prophet say this, of himself or of some other man?' Then Philip opened his mouth, and beginning at this Scripture, preached Jesus to him" (8:34-35, NKJV).

For the eunuch, this passage was where He first learned of His Savior. It was where He first realized there was a God-sent sacrifice who died so His sins could be washed away. This passage was the motivation which led to his active confession and baptism and his continual rejoicing.

As we come to the Lord's Table, it is an opportunity to remember the same joy we felt when we first learned God sent a Savior. We rejoice in the sacrifice of Jesus, our slaughtered Lamb of God, who died to take away our sins. While we are filled with great sorrow for His death, may we leave each memorial with a feeling of joy as we go through our week knowing we are forgiven through Him.

MEDITATION 47

Jesus, a Ransom Offering

In Matthew 20, Jesus contrasts the self-seeking nature of James and John, the sons of Zebedee, with his own selfless sacrifice. In verses 27 and 28 He offers some advice for those who would seek to be great in His kingdom:

> "And whoever desires to be first among you, let him be your slave— just as the Son of Man did not come to be served, but to serve, and to give His life a ransom for many" (Matthew 20:27-28).

In this passage, Jesus summarizes His ultimate purpose in coming to earth: "to serve, and to give His life a ransom for many" (v. 28). The term "ransom" is not used often in the New Testament text. We can understand more of its meaning by looking at how it was used in other ancient literature.

First, ransom was used with reference to captives of war. In order to release these captives, a ransom price would be paid to their enemy captors so these POW's might come home (*Barnes' Notes*).

Secondly, ransom was used with reference to slaves. Someone might pay the slave-owner a ransom price so the slaves might be emancipated and set free (*Robertson's Word Pictures*).

These historical pictures are also woven into mankind's redemption history. Jesus quotes Isaiah when He proclaims His mission is "to proclaim liberty to the captives" (Luke 4:18). It is Satan who has captured us. It is God who has made special amends to release us. Similarly, Paul refers to our pre-conversion life as one of spiritual enchainment. He writes, "But God be thanked that though you were slaves of sin, yet you obeyed from the heart that form of doctrine to which you were delivered" (Romans 6:17).

Spiritually, we were all once captives and slaves. Yet Jesus paid the ransom price. He did so not with money or gold, but, by the precious blood of His own life for ours. This picture was long prophesied about in the words of Isaiah and it is this ransom we celebrate as freed fugitives and as exempted prisoners. Thank God it pleased the Lord to make His soul an offering for sin—our sin.

> "And they made His grave with the wicked—
> But with the rich at His death,
> Because He had done no violence,
> Nor was any deceit in His mouth.
> Yet it pleased the Lord to bruise Him;
> He has put Him to grief.
> When You make His soul an offering for sin,
> He shall see His seed, He shall prolong His days,
> And the pleasure of the Lord shall prosper in His hand."
> (Isaiah 53:9-10)

MEDITATION 48

Jesus, Our Sin-Bearer

The word "bear" is used 107 times in the New Testament. Often, it is used with reference to a load we take upon ourselves. Consider a few examples:

- "Whoever does not **bear his own cross** and come after me cannot be my disciple" (Luke 14:27).

- "By this my Father is glorified, that you **bear much fruit** and so prove to be my disciples" (John 15:8).

- "We who are strong have an obligation to **bear with the failings** of the weak, and not to please ourselves" (Romans 15:1).

- "**Love bears all things**, believes all things, hopes all things, endures all things" (1 Corinthians 13:7).

- "**Bear one another's burdens**, and so fulfill the law of Christ" (Galatians 6:2).

- "with all humility and gentleness, with patience, **bearing with one another** in love" (Ephesians 4:2).

These are only a few instances where the New Testament speaks of our need to bear a burden for the sake of the kingdom. Yet, who is our ultimate source and example of such burden-bearing? We could go all the way back to the Isaiah text where we see the prophet foreshadowing the death of the righteous Servant who bore the sin of many.

"He shall see the labor of His soul, and be satisfied.
By His knowledge My righteous Servant shall justify many,
For He shall bear their iniquities.

Therefore I will divide Him a portion with the great,
And He shall divide the spoil with the strong,
Because He poured out His soul unto death,
And He was numbered with the transgressors,
And He bore the sin of many,
And made intercession for the transgressors."
(Isaiah 53:11-12)

As we come to the book of Hebrews, we see a direct reference to this Isaiah passage. By this reference we receive another divine confirmation about the fulfillment of the Isaiah prophecy in Jesus Christ. Hebrews 9:27-28, "And as it is appointed for men to die once, but after this the judgment, so Christ was offered once to bear the sins of many. To those who eagerly wait for Him He will appear a second time, apart from sin, for salvation."

It was Jesus who took the burden of our sins upon Himself on the cross. He bore the ultimate load for our salvation. Thus, we memorialize the burden He chose to bear on the cross each Lord's Day. Furthermore, we use the memory of His burden to go about our daily lives bearing our load and the load of others for their good and for their benefit. May we thank Jesus for His ultimate example of burden-bearing for us so we might be equipped to live a life of selfless service for others.

MEDITATION 49

Jesus Frees the Bound

In Luke 4:21, Jesus applied the prophecy of Isaiah 61 to Himself. The text says,

> "The Spirit of the Lord God is upon Me,
> Because the Lord has anointed Me
> To preach good tidings to the poor;
> He has sent Me to heal the brokenhearted,
> To proclaim liberty to the captives,
> And the opening of the prison to those who are bound;
>
> To proclaim the acceptable year of the Lord,
> And the day of vengeance of our God;
> To comfort all who mourn,
>
> To console those who mourn in Zion,
> To give them beauty for ashes,
> The oil of joy for mourning,
> The garment of praise for the spirit of heaviness;
> That they may be called trees of righteousness,
> The planting of the Lord, that He may be glorified."
> (Isaiah 61:1-3)

In a passage of beautiful phrases, take a moment to focus on just one in this passage which poetically pictures what Jesus has done for us. Verse 1 declares the Messiah is responsible for "the opening of the prison to those who are bound."

This phrase is one of newfound freedom for a prisoner who has endured deserved punishment. In our society, prisoners are surrounded by barbed wire and armed guards. They are confined to a locked cell with the most rudimentary essentials. That cell is often shared with another fellow prisoner. If any travel takes place, they are often handcuffed to avoid escape or harm. Just contemplating being a prisoner is a situation most would want to avoid or never want to remember. It is a situation of overwhelming fear.

Yet spiritually, we have all been prisoners of sin. Sin ultimately leads us to an ugly place—an eternal hell as the result of our rebellion against the Governor of our world. Yet Jesus did something for us to release us from prison. He died so we might be released and granted eternal freedom accompanied by peaceful relief. Jesus says in John 8:34-36,

> "Jesus answered them, 'Most assuredly, I say to you, whoever commits sin is a slave of sin. And a slave does not abide in the house forever, but a son abides forever. Therefore if the Son makes you free, you shall be free indeed.'"

Take a moment to think of how wonderful it is for the prisoner to be unshackled, outside of the prison yard, and to breathe in the fresh air of freedom. Yet the earthly prisoner's freedom is only as long as the rest of his life. The freedom Christ offers, by comparison, is forever. As we partake of this Lord's Supper, may we contemplate how wonderful it will be to freely roam and breathe in the fresh air of heaven someday—all because of what our Lord has done to free us.

MEDITATION 50

Jesus Offers Reconciliation for Iniquity

One of the most hurtful but needful phrases to hear is when someone says, "I'm disappointed in you." It indicates a loss of favor and a shameful breach in relationship.

On the other hand, one of the most hopeful and helpful phrases we might hear is when a person says, "I forgive you. Let's be friends again." It opens the door to moving forward. It causes us to be optimistic about the future and renews a broken relationship.

Reconciliation is a picture of that process in our spiritual lives. Our sins are a disappointing matter to God. His disfavor should cause us to be personally disappointed in ourselves. Yet through Jesus, the road to reconciliation and restored favor is paved.

In the book of Daniel, the prophet looked ahead to when the Messiah would "make an end of sins, to make reconciliation for iniquity, to bring in everlasting righteousness, to seal up vision and prophecy, and to anoint the Most Holy" (Daniel 9:24). Several promises are made in this prophecy regarding Daniel's people (Israel) and city (Jerusalem).

The New Testament helps us to see Daniel 9:24's fulfillment in Jesus, who:

• made an end of sins (Hebrews 2:14-15; 10:1-4, 12; 8:12).

• made reconciliation for iniquity (Romans 5:6-10; 2 Corinthians 5:17; Ephesians 2:11-22).

- brought in everlasting righteousness (Romans 10:4; 3:21-31; 2 Corinthians 5:21)

- sealed up vision and prophecy (Hebrews 1:1-2; John 16:13; Jude 3; Revelation 10:7)

- was anointed as the Most Holy (Hebrews 1:8-9; 10:19-22; Acts 2:25-36)

In Jesus, the thrill of reconciliation was made real. Paul even calls His work as a minister of Jesus Christ the ministry of reconciliation. It is the process of bringing lost sinners back into favor with God. Paul writes:

> "Now all things are of God, who has reconciled us to Himself through Jesus Christ, and has given us the ministry of reconciliation, that is, that God was in Christ reconciling the world to Himself, not imputing their trespasses to them, and has committed to us the word of reconciliation. Now then, we are ambassadors for Christ, as though God were pleading through us: we implore you on Christ's behalf, be reconciled to God. For He made Him who knew no sin to be sin for us, that we might become the righteousness of God in Him" (2 Corinthians 5:18-21).

As we gather at the Lord's Table to call to remembrance what the Lord has done, may we remember what we were before Jesus came and offered Himself for us. May we take a moment to remember the shame and regret of sin so that the joy and thrill of forgiveness, and renewed relationship with God can lead our hearts to thankfulness in the presence of the one who enables us to be made righteous.

MEDITATION 51

Jesus Rescues Us From the Power of the Grave

What are your thoughts as you stand at the edge of a grave? What goes through your mind as the casket is placed over the top of the rectangular, earthen hole soon to be filled with dirt? Is your mind filled with hopeless dread as if this were the final resting place of the deceased? Or is your mind filled with hopeful victory as you contemplate the future resurrection of the dead and eternity in heaven?

Hopefully, the latter thought is one which can offer you comfort and peace as you think of the reality of death. This hope is not just a wishful and baseless dream. It is based on a factual event in history which gives us a confident expectation for a future repeat in our own lives. In 1 Corinthians 15, Paul refers to this factual event in great, logical detail as he writes of the fundamental hope found in the resurrection of Jesus. Because of the resurrection, the grave no longer must be feared. Jesus overcame it. His disciples will also overcome death and live eternally.

To offer hope to the apostle's readers he quotes from an Old Testament prophet, Hosea. Hosea makes reference to God's prediction to ransom His people from the power of the grave and to be the Conqueror of death and the grave.

> "I will ransom them from the power of the grave;
> I will redeem them from death.
> O Death, I will be your plagues!
> O Grave, I will be your destruction!
> Pity is hidden from My eyes."
> (Hosea 13:14)

As Paul writes to Corinth, he speaks of this prophecy as having been fulfilled in Jesus Christ. He writes:

"O Death, where is your sting? O Hades, where is your victory?

The sting of death is sin, and the strength of sin is the law. But thanks be to God, who gives us the victory through our Lord Jesus Christ" (1 Corinthians 15:55-57).

Because of Jesus, we do not need to approach death with fear. He arose a victor from the grave. We do not need to think we have been conquered by sin and death. No—through Jesus, we have been given "the victory through our Lord Jesus Christ" (1 Corinthians 15:57). For this reason, we approach Him with thankfulness as we memorialize His death and hope-filled resurrection in this memorial. We continue to do so weekly till He comes to raise us up with Him (1 Corinthians 11:26).

MEDITATION 52

Jesus, a Fountain for Sin and Uncleanness

Zechariah 13:1 presents a clear and striking prophecy looking ahead to the death of Jesus as a propitiation for our sin. Zechariah writes, "In that day a fountain shall be opened for the house of David and for the inhabitants of Jerusalem, for sin and for uncleanness..." (Zechariah 13:1). Notice a few details from this verse which look ahead to the blood Jesus shed for mankind on the cross.

First of all, it is worthy to note this source of cleansing is likened to a fountain. The inspired writer could have used the term bucket, pool, pond or cistern, but all of these water sources can run dry. Fountains continue to flow. Often, the person and blood of Jesus Christ is referred to as a fountain of water in the New Testament (John 7:38; Revelation 7:17). The fact the inspired writer uses this term is indicative of the fullness and abundance of the sacrifice—the blood of Jesus is abundantly available to all like a fountain ever-flowing (Hebrews 9:11-15, 28; Romans 3:21-26; Ephesians 1:7-8).

Secondly, Zechariah also tells us why a fountain needed to be opened—for sin and for uncleanness. Fountains are often used for cleansing and this foreshadowed fountain was for spiritual cleansing. As we gather around the Lord's Table we are often reminded of those words of Jesus at the first Lord's Supper when He said, "This is My blood of the new covenant, which is shed for many for the remission of sins," (Matthew 26:28). His blood was shed so the sinner could receive forgiveness (Romans 6:2-3, 17). This included the house of David but also people of all nations (Amos 9:11-12; Mark 16:15-16).

But finally, Zechariah even prophesies more specifically about who would die so this fountain could be opened. Notice Zechariah 13:7:

> "'Awake, O sword, against My Shepherd, Against the Man who is My Companion,' says the Lord of hosts.
>
> 'Strike the Shepherd, And the sheep will be scattered; Then I will turn My hand against the little ones.'"

At the arrest of Jesus, Peter wanted to fight back and prevent Jesus from being unjustly crucified. Yet Jesus knew He would need to be struck. God had prepared a sword for His Son to provide a Savior to make us sons of God. John 18:11, "So Jesus said to Peter, "Put your sword into the sheath. Shall I not drink the cup which My Father has given Me?" Thank God He was indeed betrayed by His companion, Judas. Because on that day the ever-flowing stream of forgiveness was opened to all through the precious blood of Jesus Christ. May we reflect on His incredible sacrifice as we drink from His precious blood in this Memorial Supper.

MEDITATION 53

Jesus, Better Than the Angels

In Psalm 8, the psalmist looks to the massive expanse of the heavens and humbly asks, "What is man that You are mindful of him, And the son of man that You visit him?...You have made him to have dominion over the works of Your hands; You have put all things under his feet, All sheep and oxen—Even the beasts of the field..." (Psalm 8:4, 6-7).

Truly, it is amazing to contemplate that our majestic, powerful Creator God knows us down to the very hairs of our head (Luke 12:7) and cares for us. It is more touching to think that though man has sinned God still loves us and has even given us a special role as having dominion above all the animals upon the earth. Why man? Why is such divine favor bestowed upon us rather than upon another one of God's creatures? The psalmist is awed by the very thought of God's elevated concern for mankind.

Yet the Hebrew author takes the thought of the psalmist a step further as he writes of Jesus Christ and quotes this text. Just after quoting Psalm 8:6-7 he writes,

> "You have put all things in subjection under his feet.
>
> For in that He put all in subjection under him, He left nothing that is not put under him. But now we do not yet see all things put under him. But we see Jesus, who was made a little lower than the angels, for the suffering of death crowned with glory and honor, that He, by the grace of God, might taste death for everyone" (Hebrews 2:8-9).

This inspired author is not just awed that God chose man to reign over the animal creation, but that He chose to come in human flesh and now reigns over all creation (see also Philippians 2:5-11). God has granted to Jesus an even greater realm of dominion than was ever bestowed upon any mortal. The Jesus who was made a little lower than the angels while on earth is now crowned above all and has become much better than the angels as all are in subjection to him (Hebrews 1:4; 2:8).

With this New Testament reference, the eighth Psalm is not merely reflective but also prophetic. It looks ahead to that great moment where God gives dominion to His entire creation—even the angels—to His Son, the Word who became flesh (John 1:14). The first Adam had total dominion but lost it; the last Adam has complete dominion and will reign on an eternal throne. He is "Lord of lords and King of kings" (Revelation 17:14). Yet, He could only be exalted to such a position if He were willing to be humbled. Thus, as we partake of this Supper, we remember the Lord who was willing to taste death for everyone. But more importantly, we rejoice in One who proved by His resurrection not even the powers of death were too great a foe to be defeated. May the thought of the psalmist echo in our minds as we think of the sacrificial love of Jesus for sinful man while we also ask, "What is man that you were mindful of Him?"

Made in the USA
Las Vegas, NV
05 April 2024

88270148R00066